The Possibilities of

ONENESS

*Doorways to Life's Deeper
Meaning, Wonder, and Joy*

Will Irons

Copyright © 2018 William M. Irons

All rights reserved. No part of this book may be used, reproduced, translated, electronically stored, or transmitted in any manner whatsoever without prior written permission from the publisher, except by reviewers, who may quote brief passages in their reviews and certain other noncommercial uses permitted by copyright law.

For information, questions, or comments, contact:
Wisdom Wellspring Publishing
Website: WillIrons.com or Wisdomwellspringpublishing.com
Email: WillIronsBooks@gmail.com

Library of Congress Control Number: 2017918121
ISBN: 978-0-9995166-0-7
10 9 8 7 6 5 4 3 2 1

Printed in the United States of America.

Disclaimer

The information and insights in this book are solely the opinion of the author and should not be considered as a form of therapy, advice, direction, diagnosis, and/or treatment of any kind. This information is not a substitute for medical, psychological, or other professional advice, counseling, or care. All matters pertaining to your individual health should be supervised by a physician or appropriate healthcare practitioner. Neither the author nor the publisher assumes any responsibility or liability whatsoever on behalf of any purchaser or reader.

Cover and interior design: Illumination Graphics

Dedication

To all those impassioned, open-minded, and big-hearted human
beings courageous enough to explore the great unknown,
to delve into the deeper mysteries and questions of Life,
and who were drawn to share that wisdom of Oneness
with the rest of us.

Contents

Introduction 1
~ Sugar Cubes Are Not Candy! The Rest of the Story 6

Chapter 1—What Is Oneness? 13
~ Experiences of Oneness—The Beginning of Possibility 13
~ An Emerging Picture of Oneness 15
~ Consciousness and Awareness 18
~ Oneness and Its Different Meanings 20
~ Lived Oneness—The World's Wisdom Traditions 22
~ One Ocean, Many Waves—A Metaphor 24
~ Clearing the Clouded Wave—Taking the Metaphor Further 26

Chapter 2—Life's Turning Points 31
~ The Magic of Lake Echo 31
~ The Love of Wild Things 34
~ The Teachings of a Yaqui Shaman 36
~ My Universe Continues to Expand 38
~ A Jolt to My Worldview 39
~ One of the Herd and Back to Panama 40

Chapter 3—Degrees of Oneness 43
~ The Ego State—A Separate Self 44
~ The Flow State 46
~ The Wonder State 48
~ High Peak Experiences 50
~ Cosmic Consciousness—Total Unitive Consciousness 52
~ What Unity Experiences Share and What They Are Not 52

Chapter 4—Experiences of Oneness from My Life 55
Part One: One with the Living Ocean 58
~ A Second Taste 58
~ The Big Island 61
    Humpback Wonder 61
    The Sacred Valley 63
    A Circle of Rays 65
    Dolphins—Spinner's Play 67
~Panama 70
    Shark's Island 70
    Millions of Minnows 73

Part Two: Discovering Oneness at the Edge ... 75
- Glacier's Giant Surprise ... 76
- Riding on Perfect Circles ... 79
- Slide! ... 82
- Waves of Ecstasy ... 88
  - *The Meeting* ... 88
  - *The Beauty of Place* ... 92
  - *Oneness in Waves* ... 93
  - *The Finger, the Moon, and Liquid Bliss* ... 97
- Climb to Flow, Flow to Climb ... 99

Part Three: Drawn to Life and to the Power of Wild Places ... 104
- One with the Pack ... 105
- Tree Reveler ... 109
- Gardening the Cosmos ... 112
- Wild Places ... 115
  - *Coral Reefs* ... 115
  - *The Rainforest* ... 117
  - *The Big Wild* ... 119
  - *Hot Springs* ... 121

Part Four: Oneness Close to Home ... 123
- Two Waves Become One ... 123
- Rhythmic Union—Music and Dance ... 129
- Art and Artist, Two yet One ... 132
- Oneness Revealed in Life's Paths ... 134
  - *The Nurse* ... 136
  - *The Teacher* ... 138
- Walking to Oneness ... 140

Chapter 5—Oneness as Understood and Experienced by Others . 143

Chapter 6—Thirteen Circles of Timeless Wisdom ... 155
- Waking Up and Growing Up ... 155
- Thirteen Circles of Timeless Wisdom ... 159
  - *The Cosmic Kaleidoscope* ... 196
- Living the Wisdom ... 199

Chapter 7—The End That Is a Beginning ... 201

Notes ... 207
Acknowledgments ... 211
About the Author ... 213

Introduction

It was the early 1970s right around Christmastime when the unthinkable happened. Only six years old and I mistakenly ate an enormous dose of LSD. What I had thought was a plain and boring piece of candy turned out to be a hallucinogenic-loaded sugar cube. It was an unintentional leap into a cosmic rabbit hole, and that was only the beginning. Of course, there is much more to the story, but that will come shortly.

What I will say now is I am tremendously grateful that what followed after accidentally eating the psychedelic sugar cube did not end up being a regrettable story of ER chaos or freaked-out, traumatized parents (my parents had no idea what had happened until years later). On the contrary, that strange and unforgettable day set into motion many intertwining ripples of meaning and influence that continue to affect the direction of my life to this day.

It has taken nearly thirty years to arrive at a complete and expressible understanding of what occurred, to recognize how it has changed me, and finally to find a way to articulate and make sense of its broader and deeper implications. By opening the door to the unfathomable—what can only be referred to as "Infinity"—I was given a lasting taste of Universal Oneness. A seed was planted, one that would subtly call to me the rest of my life. From that moment onward, burned deeply and indelibly into the heart of my young being, was a stirring sense of mystery, of wonder, and an unflagging desire to know more.

Eventually, I was inspired to write down some of the life-changing experiences and insights that I have had since that remarkable day. The end result is the book you hold before you—*The Possibilities of Oneness*. What does it actually mean to have an experience of Oneness? What do those experiences look and feel like from a personal perspective, as well as from other people's points of view? To answer those questions, I share the realizations of Oneness from my own life experiences, as well as the invaluable, timeless wisdom that has emerged from countless human beings who have had similar types of experiences known by many different names: peak, flow or in-the-zone experiences, higher love, mystical, liberation, enlightenment, awakening, nondual, deep-religious, or spiritual experiences.

Most of us have heard one or two of these expressions; words that point to those possibilities of consciousness that often lie untapped during the busyness of our day-to-day lives. Throughout the rest of the book I will refer to these openings and unifying shifts in consciousness as "experiences of Oneness," "possibilities of Oneness," "unity experiences," or some other version of those phrases.

One of my intentions for writing this book was to attempt to describe these kinds of experiences in a way that make them seem less abstract or nebulous and more extraordinarily ordinary. I see unity experiences as incredibly potent pathways for human growth and transformation. In those moments of transcendence and Oneness, we rediscover our original common ground, our deeper natures, and our greater potentials. As I have come to understand it, unity experiences are not strictly one-of-a-kind, all-or-nothing events, or only within the reach of a select few. In reality, there is a wide and varied range of these types of experiences potentially available to all of us. The possibilities of Oneness can be discovered in simple day-to-day activities, during more complex or risky pursuits—or anywhere in between.

The insights and the collective wisdom I write about here derive from a genuinely heartfelt desire to know myself and to share with others a vision that arises out of and is rooted in a growing understanding of the bigger picture. And by "bigger picture" I mean the larger, profounder perspective that emerges from asking questions about life that explore its greater wholeness, interconnectivity, and meaning. By asking such questions over and over, in different ways, what has slowly crystallized is a clearer grasp of what experiences of Oneness are and what they might mean in the grand scheme of things. I see much more clearly now the power these possibilities have to transform our lives like nothing else.

The personal stories that people share about their realizations and intuitions into the Oneness and deeper meanings of life have been invaluable clues for helping make sense of my own unfolding. For me, those parts of any person's story are usually the most interesting and inspiring. Knowledge that is conveyed without the telling of the experiential details that led one to a fuller and richer understanding of life can often feel difficult to relate to; it is just information. That is, in fact, one of the primary motivations for sharing my personal stories here and one of the overriding reasons for writing this book: to describe in a clear and relatable way some of those lived experiences of Oneness that I see as potentialities for all of us. In fact, the greater part of this book is just that—the stories, the intimate details of my own openings to Oneness.

And to be clear, my purpose is not to discuss the experiences of Oneness that might be triggered by ingesting hallucinogenic substances; that is only one possible path of several, and ultimately a limited one in terms of long-term growth and evolution. In the short run, and on occasion, it is one way to "shake and loosen things up," but without experienced and wise guidance, the larger, imbedded meanings to be discovered from those kinds of experimentations will often be missed, misunderstood, or lost. That was certainly the case with the highly unusual circumstances of the sugar cube. It wasn't until much later in life that I finally was able to figure out the significance of that experience on my own.

Further, as much as possible, I have attempted to stay away from identifying with the specific beliefs of any particular religion or spiritual tradition when explaining my views on unity experiences. Instead, my aim has been to describe in as straightforward language as possible, free of cultural or religious baggage, some of those foundational elements of unitive wisdom found in all spiritual traditions. I am simply reinterpreting that wisdom in my own unique way, based on my own experiences and understanding, with the hope that it will be of value to the reader in ways seen and unseen.

Aside from a couple of exceptional philosophy professors, there have not been many flesh and blood teachers of the wisdom of Oneness in my life. My most valuable and ever-present teachers have been life, the inner wisdom we all share, relationships, consistent meditation, deep questioning, self-reflection through writing and contemplation, along with countless books. Like many spiritual journeys, mine has at times been a convoluted one, but to me it is those twists and turns that have made it so interesting. The important part is that it is a journey that has evolved out of my own choices and intuitions. For in the end, life itself—more than anything else—will always be our most illuminating and persistent teacher.

The roadways that might lead us to a vaster panoramic view of Oneness are varied and many. Others can offer us glimpses into their experiences and realizations; they can share their insights and understandings—but only up to a point. Ultimately we must make our own way, create our own pathways, discover and live our own truths.

I have always had a strong yearning to walk my own path of spiritual growth and transformation—free of the dictates, control, or rules of another given or supposed authority. The fulfilling road for me has been and continues to be discovering and living the kernels of unitive knowledge to be found in many of the world's wisdom traditions and making that wisdom my own—not by creating a smorgasbord, a little of this and a little of that, but by creating a cohesive, integrative whole of life-guiding wisdom. How did I do that? I describe the process in Chapter 6: "Thirteen Circles of Timeless Wisdom."

The overall flow of the remaining sections of the book will begin with a brief but crucially important explanation of what unity experiences are in a general sense, how they can be defined, along with a well-known metaphor for envisioning Oneness and its relationship to the many. That piece, Chapter 1, is the foundation and ground work for understanding the rest of the book. From there, I paint a picture of the key life events that led me to discover and finally write the possibilities of Oneness, followed by a short description of how I have come to see unity experiences as lying along a spectrum of deepening degrees of Oneness. This then leads into the heart of the book—the unity experiences themselves, ending with the Thirteen Circles of Timeless Wisdom mentioned above.

I offer no final answers in this book, no set-in-stone method or path for discovering these possibilities of consciousness. Instead I share suggestions, examples, lived experiences, and words of wisdom from others. I in no way claim to have achieved some kind of final enlightenment or awakening—something I don't feel actually happens very often. Depending on our circumstances, desires, and priorities, we are all to greater or lesser degrees in a continual and ongoing process of waking up and enlightening. It is the possibility of rediscovering who we are underneath what we have always been told and what we continually tell ourselves.

Each of us possesses the inborn potential and tendency to grow into expanding, more inclusive and unifying spheres of consciousness. It is the inevitable growth and evolution that is gleaned from the act of living itself—from experience. That, to me, is the beauty and wisdom of life, especially a self-reflective, inspired life lived with vision, authenticity, and with presence.

Sugar Cubes Are Not Candy!
The Rest of the Story

Like many six-year-old kids, I had a driving desire for sugar. If I couldn't find candy or some other sugar-enriched delight in the house, I would hunt for wayward change so that I could go to a nearby vending machine. After inserting the coins and pressing the coded, illuminated buttons, I would wait excitedly for that never-disappointing "clunk" that would echo in the mouth of the great machine as the brightly colored package hit bottom. With eager expectancy I'd watch as the metal corkscrew unwound slowly to release its mouthwatering dose of sugar. Mr. Pavlov would have been proud.

This day was different however—very different. For some reason, I began searching in the depths of my parents' densely cluttered closet for hidden treats. I don't remember ever having found candy there before. So why I looked for it on that particular day, in that rather odd place, I can't say. Perhaps I had developed enough of a sugar junkie's finely honed ability to detect the presence of hidden sugar molecules and I just knew.

I approached the shadowy closet with no clear idea of where to look or what exactly I thought I might find. I simply began rummaging through piles of clothes, shoeboxes, bags, drawers, and anything else that looked like it held promise. Though there was no light in the closet that I could find, enough ambient light entered from the bedroom for me to continue the hunt. In some strange way, the fort-like feeling and low light was comforting, along with that faint musty smell of old clothes, shoes, and leather.

Close to giving up after searching fruitlessly for several minutes, some pantyhose hanging on a hook near the closet door caught my attention. Logically, for a six-year-old anyway, I reached inside the pantyhose and began searching for some imagined sweet. Maybe the pantyhose resembled Christmas stockings just enough; it was the season, and I knew there had to be candy stashed away somewhere.

My kiddy intuition paid off. In the bottom of the pantyhose, where my mother's big toe would have fit, I found a curious lump of something neatly wrapped in tinfoil. Naturally I opened it; it had to be good if it was hidden that well. Lucky me: a single, perfectly shaped cube of sugar. So I ate it. It was sweet like I expected it to be, even without color. But there was something different about this cube; unbeknownst to me, it contained a Timothy Leary-size dose of LSD! Needless to say, my day changed considerably.

Some of the more vivid impressions I recall are centered on being completely enthralled and enchanted by shapes, textures, and colors—in whatever form I happened to encounter them. It was as if the world as a whole and everything in it was suddenly and vibrantly alive, glowing from within, lucid, radiant, and speaking to me in a silent language only I understood. All that I sensed, all that I touched seemed to be full of life and vitality, animated with pulsating energy.

The Christmas tree with its jungle of decorations took on a whole new meaning. I spent hours immersed in a magical world of colors and blinking lights, as the delicious smells of the holiday season wafted about me. Transfixed, I stared at the glass bulbs' shifting reflections and was enamored by all the small creatures—the elves, the reindeer, and the snowmen—all in marvelous costumes waiting patiently for my attentions. The tree and all that it contained was a newly awakened world of living light that I was somehow connected to. Even at that age it was fascinating to see in this way, to be able to sense that there is life and energy in "everything."

Despite the strangeness of this new experience, there was no fear or even much confusion as to why things had suddenly changed the way they had. I wasn't afraid of what was happening because I hadn't had enough life experiences to know what I should be fearful of—other than the few obvious dangers we are all taught to be aware of like playing with matches or forgetting to look both ways before crossing a busy street. At that age a child has no real conceptual framework from which to interpret or judge an experience of that kind, so I flowed with the day as if it was just another very interesting and exciting adventure. I was definitely a curious kid, and this was simply fuel for the fire.

The truly unforgettable, metamorphic part of the experience though came at the end of the day, under a night sky that felt like a bottomless sea of darkness, pulsing with a maze of star fire. And I know well that words can't possibly convey the full wonder of what I felt and experienced next. It is that same feeling that anyone feels when attempting to describe those "beyond words and outside of time" experiences. Nevertheless, here's what happened.

I had been running around the neighborhood exploring the new sensation of aliveness that was everywhere and in everything, feeling an incredible lightness and exuberant wildness. As I was walking up the sidewalk toward our townhouse, I began staring intently up into the immensity of stars and space. Suddenly I started experiencing the startling sensation of my body becoming lighter and lighter by the moment. It felt as if all that was "me" was being shed—layer by layer. This physical body that I knew as "Billy" began losing its normal sense of boundedness; my young and still-forming identity felt like it was slowly but surely opening up, spreading out, releasing, and filling the night sky. I can still remember the feeling so clearly and perfectly. The simple awareness that remained continued to expand effortlessly upward and outward, weightless and free, as if the universe was lifting my awareness, now liberated from "me," with infinite, unseen hands. There was no apprehension or thoughts of resistance, only innocent surrender.

I had become everything—and nothing. My body was still there obviously; I didn't literally disappear or dissolve into nothingness. But my consciousness had broken through the boundaries and limits of body, mind, and self and was soaring into Mystery. The timeless, boundless awareness, energy, and being that I am in truth merged with and returned to the Infinite. I was truly one with the Universe, but more than that, I *was* the Universe, and that Infinity from which the universe arises—*Oneness*. There was no I, no me, no identity, no self, no Billy; there was only crystal clear, unlimited awareness, an infinite field of pure energy and potential that is the source of all that exists. This is our truth, our essence—the wonder, bliss, and miracle of consciousness and being. I had returned home.

A feeling or experience of Oneness is "awareness" in its most essential and purest form. It is a taste of who and what we are in our depths, underneath our many thought-generated coverings, our many roles and identities. Given my young age at the time of the sugar-cube incident, along with my relative freedom from limiting preconceptions and beliefs about reality, those "coverings" were fewer and my "underneath" was much closer at hand.

The little thinking that did occur during the experience was basic and mostly navigational in nature. It had a minimal influence in terms of filtering, changing, or shaping the experience overall, especially during the deeper state of Oneness that took place at the end of the day. Instead, I was living and feeling what was unfolding fully in the now, directly and without thought or alarm. The usual limiting boundaries of my young self dropped easily allowing the within and without to become transparent and one.

The memory of this experience is so deeply etched in my mind, heart, and body; it has always felt as if it just happened. I have no memory issues. The challenging part, due to the ineffable nature of the experience itself, is describing what unfolded so that it makes sense. Unity experiences are direct and pure in nature, bypassing the filtering and shaping effects of thoughts, words, and concepts—meaning they are not like ordinary experiences where fragmenting thought processes, reality-shaping beliefs, and discriminating judgments are normally our primary modes of interpreting reality. I didn't need to use words or hold special thoughts and beliefs for this experience to happen. This was a possibility of Oneness that came spontaneously and of its own accord, encouraged, but not guaranteed, by the heightened consciousness brought out by the LSD.

I don't remember the exact moment or year that I fully realized what had happened with the sugar cube. Most of it finally fell together during the end of high school and into college. I do recall one particular light-bulb moment during high school when it suddenly came to me that I had had a remarkable experience and it had something to do with the sugar cube. But it took years to comprehend the full meaning of the event, to put it all together to the point where I could write about it. I certainly have no regrets that this particular life changer happened to me. Although extremely unlikely—it might have gone bad; I may have ended up crazier than normal. But to be honest, I'm all right with a little healthy craziness in my life.

You might ask why a megadose of acid was in our house in the first place and hidden in such an odd place? I asked my mother about it several years ago to see if she remembered anything. After a few minutes of listening to me describe what had happened, a wide-eyed shock of recognition flashed on her face. I don't recall her exact words, but it was something along the lines of "How could you have possibly found that?!" She went on to explain that a friend had given her the sugar cube to try, but she was too terrified to take it. So she hid it in the one place where she was sure no one would ever find it—except for me, of course.

Why didn't she just throw the sugar-cube away or wash it down the drain? I'm guessing she was too afraid to do that as well—not knowing where it might end up or what havoc it could wreak elsewhere. In defense of my mother, she was only in her early twenties when all this happened. She was a young woman in the seventies, when experimenting with psychedelic drugs was still the rage. Her friend simply wanted to include her in the times. In the end, she did what she thought was best, underestimating the sneakiness of her sugar-obsessed son.

Before writing about this part of the story, I asked for her permission to tell her unplanned part in the sugar-cube episode. Absolutely not, she said. More than once, I asked her to explain her resistance, and the answer was usually the same—vague. She responded mostly with what seemed to be the fear of long-overdue consequences and the massive wave of disapproval that would follow once the word got out.

So I agreed to her request—for a while—until I realized that it would leave a gaping hole in the story and a semi-important question unanswered. I told her it was too late for the acid police to come after her, and fortunately, after some prodding and begging, she overcame her reluctance and finally gave me the go ahead. We still chuckle about it.

/ Chapter 1
What Is Oneness?

> *"A human being is a part of the whole, called by us Universe, a part limited in time and space. He experiences himself, his thoughts and feelings as something separate from the rest—a kind of optical delusion of his consciousness."*
> —Albert Einstein

Experiences of Oneness—The Beginning of Possibility

Since that unexpected discovery of Oneness as a child, I have been strongly drawn to anything and everything that I thought might reconnect me in some way, shape, or form to that indescribable feeling. During my younger years, the way that desire was understood and how it manifested were largely subconscious and beyond my deliberate choice. As were the far-reaching effects of experience though, the right circumstances have shown up again and again at pivotal junctures in my life, allowing me to continue to unravel the profounder truths of Oneness.

Throughout the different phases of my journey, I have struggled to understand what it really means to have an experience of Oneness with something—with a place, with another person, with the universe itself. The possibility of feeling "at one" with something or having an "experience of Oneness" might at first seem unlikely and difficult to grasp because it is so different from how we normally perceive and experience the world.

I have heard it spoken of in many ways: There is the person who realizes a Oneness with Spirit, with God, or however one might conceive the greater Ultimate Reality; the lovers who become one with each other through deep presence, passion, and intimacy; the artist who drops any sense of separation with the art form unfolding—subject and object blur and merge into a felt Oneness; the musician who loses all sense of self, becomes one with the music that plays itself; the athletes who enter a state of flow, experience Oneness with the intricacies of their sport; the surfer who becomes one with and inseparable from the dynamic and unfurling energy of wind, ocean, and wave; the animal lover, the lover of life, who discovers a deep unity with another living being; or the person who feels a deep connection and sense of Oneness with nature, with the pulse and rhythm of life, with element, earth, and the cosmos.

Most of us have had at least a glimmer of those unexpected moments of awe-inspiring beauty discovered in natural settings—if only for a moment. These are those breathtaking, thought-stilling, mind-opening experiences that suddenly and often unexpectedly take hold of us, surprise us, and wake us up to a wider feeling of connectedness. They are those timeless moments when that irrepressible yearning to feel at one with the greater beyond overtakes us, becomes real, and fills our hearts with a wondrously fulfilling sense of deeper meanings and belonging. In this experience is the possibility of a vibrant aliveness that grows and reverberates with every beat of our hearts and with every breath.

Or perhaps we have a subtler encounter with Oneness: A simple act of kindness, of service, or a meaningful experience shared with another human being or group of people that allows our habitual sense of separateness to dissipate for a time, enabling love, selflessness, and Oneness to fill and unify that space instead. Other doorways into the possibilities of Oneness might also be found in the attention-focusing and rhythmic effects of purposefully directed movement or of various skilled and patterned activities that induce a feeling of "flow"—music, dance, sports, and many others.

An Emerging Picture of Oneness

The possible openings to Oneness are diverse and many. But *how* do these experiences actually happen? Part of the answer to that question has to do with the limits imposed by our constantly thinking minds and the inflexible belief that we only exist as separate beings. The challenge is that our often-overactive minds, especially conditioned, robot-like ways of thinking, can act like blinding barriers to our true potentials for entering into more unified states of awareness. That limitation is overcome though when attention is trained or spontaneously becomes focused on something other than the mind's endless thought processes.

When the fragmenting effect of thought, and the sense of separateness those thoughts create, is disengaged by rediscovering presence, our minds will often quiet naturally, and a bigger picture of Oneness will then be experienced. As we gain the skill to watch our thoughts instead of being identified with them (more about that later), we gradually learn to enter the stillness between thoughts. In this way, awareness is allowed to expand and our minds and hearts permitted to open in new and revealing ways. Without the effort and thoughts of a "me" getting in the way of what is happening in the Now, consciousness is able to open into a more inclusive and unifying awareness.

In essence, unity experiences are simply differing degrees of presence, and presence is awareness clear and free of the mind's endless activity, a return to who and what we are in the most essential and fundamental sense: pure, selfless awareness. In presence, there is a return to the here and Now, to being and to groundedness. We reawaken to the possibilities of Oneness; we finally feel the true happiness and the unequaled sense of liberation to be discovered by being unchained from the thought generated and perpetuated "idea" of a self that is often overly preoccupied with the fears and worries of a past that is gone and a future that can only be imagined.

Experiences of Oneness are an opening and moving of consciousness from separation to wholeness. Suddenly (or gradually) an expanding sense of union is felt with some aspect of the world that normally feels separate and distinct. The usual sense of being a separate self, an individual or discrete personality—what is also called "ego"—clears, is seen through, or at least diminishes. Boundaries loosen and new, sometimes unimaginable possibilities unfold. The ego, our learned sense of self, is not solid or as fixed as we have been led to believe. It is not a thing; it is a process and therefore open and malleable.

A truly unforgettable elation can emerge by letting go, even momentarily, of the seemingly unshakable feeling of being a self separate from all that is around it. By learning to intentionally direct our awareness, to simultaneously focus yet expand our attention on and beyond something other than a learned feeling of identification with thoughts, emotions, and with the sense of ego that they help to create, we begin to let go of the fears and anxiousness that often hold us back and limit our possibilities. We start to feel a sense of true freedom and joy.

We are neither our thoughts nor the egos created and sustained by those thoughts; they are only a means of creating, doing, and of interacting in the world. Our ego is not who we are in our deepest being. To the extent that we are incessantly conditioned to believe that life is all about us as separate, cutoff, and isolated selves, we are blinded to our wider capacities for genuine compassion, empathy, and love—all possibilities of Oneness. This is a hugely important realization with the potential to eliminate a tremendous amount of unnecessary, self-inflicted suffering from our lives, allowing us to experience so much more.

Reflecting back on the various experiences of Oneness I have had over the years, I realize without a doubt that those openings in awareness have been the most amazing, meaningful, and extraordinary experiences in my life. They are hints of possibility, a calling to a more expansive truth below the surface level of our usual self-important, ego-based consciousness. Underneath is a greater unity that perpetually informs and sustains us and all that exists. Unity experiences are, to varying degrees, inklings of our greater human potentialities; they are reminders of who we already and always are in essence, but have forgotten.

With our totalities—body, mind, heart, and spirit—we hunger for wholeness, love, belonging, and the meaning brought to life by those feelings. And despite how it often appears to the contrary, Oneness realized and expressed through love and creativity is, I believe, our greatest desire and the quintessential motivation behind so much of what we are, what we strive for, and how we finally act in the world. This most elementary and powerful drive for Oneness and love in our lives is what continually calls us to act and to create a greater sense of connection and completion in our lives.

On the other hand, the types of experiences and feelings we most abhor and fear in life are those unbalanced and extreme forms of what I refer to as "separative" consciousness: a distorted, discordant, and self-absorbed state of consciousness that, at its worse, can lead to severe mental, physical, emotional, and spiritual suffering—to disease, neurosis, and apathy. It is this kind of divisive and fragmenting consciousness, veiled and steeped in ignorance and misunderstanding, which can in its darkest and most deluded moments result in acts of hatred, terrorism, mass shootings, the horror of death camps, environmental destruction, and genocide. The greater a person's, a group's, a nation's, or a society's sense of separation, selfishness, alienation, and aloneness, the greater the chance for destructive acts and an uncaring disregard for ourselves and others—not only other humans, but for all other life forms and for the planet itself.

Fortunately, at some level, we are all magnetized to the bigger picture, to that which is transcendent—to an experience of life that is larger, wider, more inclusive, and embracing than what we normally perceive as our individual selves. This call to Oneness, to a genuine realization of love in the loftiest, most encompassing sense of the word, is an inherent element of being human, undeniable in its power and influence in our lives as individuals and as a whole. It is the very basis and foundation of religion and spirituality, in all their myriad expressions throughout recorded history and before. Its realization is the only way of being and acting in the world that can bring any real or lasting joy. To me this is the true meaning of "spirituality."

Consciousness and Awareness

Before going further, it is important to clarify the use of two potentially confusing words—"consciousness" and "awareness." Both words are often viewed as near equivalents, interchangeable, and each term is frequently used to define the other. Part of the reason for this circularity and ambiguity is that consciousness remains one of the greatest and most elusive mysteries of our time. Science still has no definitive answers as to what it is or how it happens, at least not from within the limitations of its mostly materialistic and reductionist approach.

Most commonly, the word "consciousness" is associated with "self-awareness," with the capacities to think and reason, to use symbols and language, to know the world in logical and self-reflective ways, to imagine and to create. It is normally viewed as a mostly human characteristic (although that belief is slowly changing). Some believe consciousness is nothing more than a biological property of life that emerges naturally out of the electrochemical activity of the brain—a shortsighted and limiting belief to be sure. Of course, many of us know intuitively that there is very likely more to the story than that and much left to be discovered.

On the other hand, what consciousness *does* can be experienced firsthand and known with more certainty. Consciousness can be envisioned as the field or screen on and through which perceptions, thoughts, feelings, ideas, and all experience are able to unfold. Without consciousness in the form of self-awareness there is no "known" experience. In a real sense, consciousness *is self-aware experience*. That being said, I will use the terms "consciousness" and "self-awareness" (or simply "awareness") as terms denoting our capacity to be self-reflective, to be aware that we are aware and to know that we know.

I have also come to imagine the word "awareness" in a larger way—as composing the fabric of the universe itself—as pure Awareness. Pure Awareness, as I see it, is primary and prior to self-awareness or consciousness; it is what makes it possible for consciousness to exist at all, in the same way a sculpture is given life, form, and meaning out of the potential of unformed clay or the way the ocean's water gives rise to the existence of waves.

Viewed in another way, pure Awareness is like an empty and open canvas while consciousness, in the form of self-awareness, allows the contents of that canvas to be known, enables the screen of consciousness to be experienced. Awareness in this big sense can be imagined as an infinite field or medium for the broadcasting and manifestation of the universe and all that it contains. And as intelligent, self-aware beings with incredibly complex and sensitive brains, we have become its conscious receivers and "experiencers."

Uncovered in this incredible process is the amazing wonder of the universe becoming conscious of itself.

Oneness and Its Different Meanings

With all of the above in mind then, how might Oneness be defined and made relevant to day-to-day life? One way to understand Oneness is to envision it as layers of meaning and degrees of possibility. As reflected throughout the natural world, gradations and measured variations are the norm in nature; experiences of Oneness are also mirrors of these differences. With that in mind, unity experiences can be seen as a spectrum, a rainbow of different potentials of experience.

A synthesis of various dictionary definitions for Oneness looks something like this: "Oneness is the fact or state of being unified or whole though seemingly composed of two or more parts." Some common synonyms for the word "Oneness" might include: singleness, integrity, wholeness, harmony, sameness, universality, indivisibility, solidarity, identity, unity, or union. Each variation possesses its own peculiar nuance of meaning.

Oneness in the above sense is a word, a concept, and a reality-shaping facet of language. It is defined (ironically) as a particular aspect of the world that we have come to divide and create boundaries around. In this way, Oneness is understood and given meaning only in relation to its opposite: the many, diversity, separateness, divided, parts, multiplicity, or duality. This is the relative meaning of Oneness—the Oneness of thought and language.

At a deeper level, Oneness could be said to be harmony, connection, union, or a sense of wholeness with someone, someplace, or something at the various levels of being—energetically, physically, emotionally, mentally, spiritually, and ecologically. This larger experience of Oneness is the beginning of feeling a sense of unity that lies outside of the constraints of thought and reason. At this level,

Oneness is a gradual and partial moving beyond opposites, beyond a strictly dualistic and conceptual relationship with the world into a purer experience of Oneness that is more direct and intuitive in nature. By "direct" I mean there is a relaxing or bypassing of the usual thoughts, beliefs, and preset ideas that can act as extremely selective and distorting filters in terms of how we interpret the world.

Once these habitual, conceptual filters are suspended through learning to live more consciously with presence and in the Now, an intuition of Oneness begins to illuminate one's life. As the constricting effect of identifying with a self-centered ego loosens its grasp and frees up our attention, awareness becomes more transparent, begins to open and expand. A sense of equanimity is gained and we start to realize with deepening conviction that it is pure spacious awareness, before thought and emotions, which is the root of who we are in truth, and the unifying matrix for all of existence.

In its grandest and most difficult-to-define sense, Oneness has no opposite. It is beyond all duality and unconditional. It is, in fact, sometimes called the "nondual" as a way to distinguish it from the relative and relational use of the word Oneness. Nondual Oneness is the paradox of paradoxes: timeless, limitless, boundless, and without conditions—existing beyond logic, language, thoughts, or concepts. Yet at the same time, it is the very source and essence of those things and of everything else.

Nondual Oneness is the nontemporal, nonspatial Source of all that is, all that has been, and all that is possible. It is the center that is all centers, everywhere and nowhere at once, an impossible-to-imagine emptiness that is the infinite wellspring of existence. According to certain theories within the field of modern cosmology, nondual Oneness is like an infinite quantum vacuum of pure potentiality that is at once "nothing" yet also "resonating and brimming" with the possibilities of all that exists. It is the "what was before" the Big Bang, from and through which the universe exploded into existence.

These riddles of language are used as a way to create an "intuition" of nondual Oneness. In the end, it can only be pointed to through symbols, metaphors, stories, and myths, or experienced directly and intuitively through unity experiences. Oneness in this largest sense is the heart of our being, our center, and home. It is the very meaning of "Uni"-verse. It is the Oneness I first experienced as a child.

Lived Oneness—The World's Wisdom Traditions

There is a worldview that sees the ultimate Oneness portrayed above as the heart and essence of our relationship to the world and cosmos. According to what is called the World's Wisdom Traditions (also referred to as the Perennial philosophy, popularized by the writer Aldous Huxley), many of the world's religions and spiritual traditions, some philosophical schools of thought, along with many of the world's Native spiritual traditions share at their roots a common foundational thread of human unitive wisdom from which they all, in different ways and with different cultural coverings, derive their original founding truths, inspiration, and meaning.

A few of these Wisdom Traditions are familiar to many of us already, given that they are at the heart of some of the world's largest religious groups. From Hinduism is the nonduality of Advaita Vedanta; from Christianity are the Mystics—the Father and I are One; from Yoga there is the "union" of body, mind, heart, and spirit; from Islam there is Sufism—knowing the Oneness of Lover and Beloved; from Judaism there is the Kabbalah—to unite intuitively with God, symbolically through the mystical center and source—The Tree of Life; from Native Traditions of the world there is Shamanism and Nature Mysticism—a deeply felt Oneness and connectedness with Nature and the Universe as One; from Sikhism there is merging with God; from Taoism there is living in harmony, in accord and as one with the indefinable Source of All—the Tao;

from Buddhism, Zen in particular, there is the direct realization of our true natures underneath the coverings of self, finally seeing through the illusion of a separate self (enlightenment) into a the greater Awareness and Wholeness that is our truth—our Buddha Natures; from the ancient Greek philosopher Plotinus, there are the NeoPlatonists who believe in the One, out of which arises the Intellect, the Forms, and the Soul.

This list is certainly not exhaustive, and it is important to keep in mind that although each of these traditions is sometimes expressed and enacted quite differently outwardly, underneath there is still a shared and common ground of Oneness.

To reiterate then, the Wisdom Traditions of the world hold that there is a greater underlying Oneness that is infinite and inconceivable in nature, the ultimate source of all that exists, all that is experienced, and of all that is known and unknown. We have come to refer to this Infinity with a multitude of names, and each speaks of the many possible and varied ways of relating to Ultimate Reality: Spirit, Oneness, Being, Source, God, Brahman, The Tao, Ultimate Reality, Emptiness, The Void, Great Mystery, Infinite Potential, Infinity, Oneness, The One, or—as I like to call it—Life, Big Life, or Infinite Life.

Each of these names, and of course there are many more, emerges from a particular cultural and historical context, along with an array of specific beliefs, feelings, and distinctive traditions associated with each. All are powerfully affecting words used to point to and create a connection to that unifying ground of existence, and each expresses a unique interpretation and understanding of the One Source. Some are more active in nature; others are more receptive, yet all are correct. They are all unique ways of peering into the same inexhaustible depths of an infinite, illuminated jewel.

Further, according to the Wisdom Traditions, it is this Oneness that is the very essence of who we are and our most profound truth. Sometimes it is referred to as our true and original nature:

transparent and spacious awareness unclouded and emptied of our mind-generated ideas of self-identity, personality, or ego. It is the "being" in human beings; it is soul or spirit, not as some immaterial, phantasmal version of the self and personality, but as pure being, energy, and awareness. And as often as we believe to the contrary, it is impossible to separate ourselves from this ground of Oneness. Attempting to do so is like trying to separate a wave from the ocean.

Whether gradual or sudden, life-altering or glimpsing, this realization of what the Wisdom Traditions refer to as our Oneness with and inseparability from the greater whole is what I am referring to when using the phrase "the possibilities of Oneness." It is through unity experiences or experiences of Oneness that we are enabled with new eyes and in different ways to see that our being and the ultimate ground of Being are one, that Life as infinite is the originating power of all finite life—one but many. As it is sometimes expressed, the One that is All and All that is One is like the rays of an infinite sun: although each ray appears separate, unique, and distinct, they are in truth all one with their source and one with each other, indivisible and whole.

Through experiences of Oneness we see that human awareness—before "self"-awareness, is simply the "I am" of our deepest being prior to our personalities, labels, and roles. And at our centers lives this ever-present, unifying continuity, an unchanging presence that is in time but timeless, limited yet infinite. It is the same essential awareness, that same familiar feeling that is always felt as our innermost being; it is with us when we are born, when we are young, with us as we grow old, and with us when we die. That is Oneness, and that is who we are.

One Ocean, Many Waves—A Metaphor

Why is the greater reality of Oneness so often described as inconceivable, as unknowable by way of logic, thoughts, and words? One of the primary reasons for that seeming elusiveness is the simple fact that any attempt to use our normal dichotomizing thought processes to break Infinity into parts is invariably doomed to failure. Attempting to scientifically explain or reduce Ultimate Reality to parts is like trying to pull a bucket of water out of a river to watch it flow, and then making statements of truth about a flowing river based on those extremely limited and distorted observations.

The key then is to find a way to point metaphorically to the indivisible relationship between the relative world of our day-to-day lives and the ultimate and absolute unified reality that is life's root and source. Having some form of analogy in place that allows us to "liken" the sometimes difficult-to-grasp idea of Oneness and experiences of Oneness to something concrete and commonly found in the world around us can be tremendously helpful.

The ocean with its waves as a tangible symbol suggestive of the Infinite is about as close as the human mind can come to grasping what it can only ever partially imagine, and for centuries it has served to represent this mutually arising relationship of the One to the many, of the Infinite to the finite. We look out on this enormous expanse of water and see a seemingly endless horizon, where boundless sea meets limitless sky. And then there are the unfathomable, mysterious depths of the ocean itself and the light that shines on for what seems like forever.

Imagine the ocean then as a visual metaphor and likeness of Infinity, of Oneness. While the waves that arise out of this infinite Ocean are simultaneously a finite yet unending, creative expression of that Oneness—of Life, Source, Spirit, God, or Being. Every wave represents a unique manifestation of the vast creative powers intrinsic to the Ocean. In other words, the Ocean is the Source of existence, while its waves are the never-ending ways that existence is manifested and expressed. And the water that forms this Ocean of Oneness with its ever-unfurling waves or reality is Pure Awareness—the empty field of potential that becomes Life's universal canvas.

What is more, all the countless waves that continually emerge from and are sustained by this boundless Ocean of Oneness are also vibrational, energetic, and informational in nature. They become the universe as we know it—the finite world of light, dimension, space, time, and extension. Every wave arising from the One Ocean becomes some aspect of the world of form, sensed and unsensed—of people, places, and things, change and transformation, everything. And just as waves possess crest and trough, so too our interpretation of the universe becomes infused with a sense of this basic duality of life: good and bad, right and wrong, me and you, subject and object, inside and outside.

Finally, although each wave is unique and appears distinct, all waves are interconnected and one with the Ocean. There are waves within waves within waves, and it is impossible to separate a wave from the ocean, or the ocean from the wave. Here again speaks the ancient wisdom at the heart of the universe: All and each in One, and One in each and All. From the largest galaxy to the smallest vibratory constituents of matter, all are expressed as waves that emerge like musical vibrations or notes in a patterned, evolving, orchestrated harmony. And eventually arising from this Universal Symphony are human waves of being; beings that have become aware that they are aware.

Clearing the Clouded Wave—Taking the Metaphor Further

From the moment we are born into the innocent awareness of a newborn, we gradually and inevitably begin to develop into the self-awareness of an adult. A plethora of molding forces are activated and begin shaping our young, malleable bodies and minds: biology, genetics, the environment, along with the many diverse socialization and enculturation influences continually shaping our lives.

Year by year we are sculpted by family, friends, teachers, by all the information, media, and technology that we are exposed to daily, as well as by unique geographical, historical, political, economic, environmental, and social circumstances. This is the beginning of self-identity, the process of individualization, the creation of separation and boundaries. The pure awareness of the newly created human wave of awareness gradually becomes "self"-aware; it is given form, limits, boundaries, and is defined. It is the formation of the I, of ego, and of the personality.

At the same time, the learning and acquisition of language and communication skills begins. Starting with body language, nuances of emotion and feeling are expressed through our physicality. From there, simple repetitive sounds emerge; slowly, and after years of unrelenting effort, those basic sounds transform into a spoken language. The root of self-identity is established in this way. Language becomes our thought stream—a constantly flowing internal dialogue that consists of beliefs, judgments, information, and all the differentiating, categorizing, and discriminating ideas that we develop about the world, about self, and about other. It is this thought stream and all the many feelings created out of that stream that becomes our self-concept.

We are all born into this seemingly real and solid world of endless things, relationships, and flux, where the underlying Oneness from which existence arises is not at once obvious. We forget the bigger picture: our true nature, our connectedness, and our inherent unity. We become lost to our true Source—the greater Ocean of Oneness from which we arise. It becomes obscured, hidden, and veiled from us. Separateness eventually feels like our primary reality. Our individual waves, instead of being transparent and clear to our true and original nature, become clouded.

The pure Awareness that we are underneath is gradually covered over by layers of belief, preconception, and conditioning. Eventually, out of habit, all these learned and separating patterns of thought act as filters that predetermine our experience to an enormous extent. The original translucent and crystalline waters of Awareness become shrouded, like the mirror that is masked by a film of water vapor.

We often end up losing the naturalness and spontaneity of a consciousness that knows its deeper connection to Life. As the inside of our individual waves becomes more and more clouded and cut off from the whole, an opaqueness forms; it gradually becomes reflective and mirror like. Soon the majority of what each of us senses, feels, and thinks becomes encapsulated and trapped by this mirroring effect, chained to the "idea" of a self that is separate from everything and everyone, absorbed and wholly identified with its own reflections.

Eventually, we begin to falsely equate who we are in our hearts with this thought-sustained sense of self, with feelings, professions, talents, family, money, power, fame, religion, culture, and things—on and on. But these are simply coverings or roles. They are all important parts of the play and genius of life and an aspect of who we are, but not our truer, profounder natures.

The forming of a self, of an ego is a natural and necessary process. It is our point of reference, our tool for navigating this dimension of space and time, form, perspective, change, and a world of billions of other humans. But it is only one stage of many possible levels of growth. If the ego stage of consciousness is not outgrown and transformed into a higher and more inclusive form of awareness, it becomes unhealthy or pathological even. It is common for this natural "self"-building process to cause us to become disconnected from the larger truths and possibilities of our beings, but the beauty of life is that it too can change and be changed.

We are "beings" who have unknowingly yet willing cut ourselves off from the greater Being and flow of Life from and through which we emerge anew moment to moment. We forget;

yet there still resides in our depths a stirring desire to return to our true home, to rediscover the wave that is one with the Ocean—our completeness. There are times, even if rare, that we intuit that we are missing something essential; we hear the omnipresent vibratory hum of the Infinite calling and it whispers to us undeniably and deeply.

What follows is a large part of that story for me.

Chapter 2
Life's Turning Points

Time and again, my life seemed to be influenced and directed by that first experience of Oneness. As I was continually driven to seek the larger meanings behind those kinds of experiences, there were specific key-life transitions essential for helping me to develop and expand my understanding of experiences of Oneness—slowly helping me to see and feel the bigger picture of Life in both its infinite and relative sense.

The Magic of Lake Echo

From the age of about six to eleven, I was fortunate to have been a part of a genuine hippie commune outside of Tampa, Florida. We lived there for a summer and then continued to visit after we moved to a house that was nearby. That first summer we slept in one of those giant green army tents, and to this day I savor that earthy, musty, canvas smell. It was during that summer and the following years at the lake that my feelings of Oneness with nature—and especially water—began emerging. If given the opportunity, most young kids have a natural propensity to develop a close and sometimes "magical" relationship with the natural world. That happened for me, but I sense that it went slightly further than it might have thanks to the sugar-cube adventure.

The commune was situated around a pristine and beautiful spring-fed lake called Lake Echo. Surrounding the lake was a scattering of old wooden houses built up off the ground in a style typical of a sometimes rainy and wet coastal environment. Back then, most of the outlying area was a dense, jungle-like swath of cypress-filled swamps, giant oaks thick with hair-like Spanish mosses, orange groves on the outskirts, and the lake itself at the center. The lake was pure, fantastical magic—crystal clear and filled with life of all kinds, moving seen and unseen in its dark, enigmatic depths. Those waters represented something intensely mysterious—and just out of reach.

I can still picture some of the people who made up Lake Echo's eclectic cast of long-haired hippies. The commune was started by a philosophy professor who wanted to establish a community of like-minded people inspired to live close to the earth and in tune with her larger rhythms. I was allowed to be a part of some of the earth-revering rituals they enacted on occasion. I still see clearly in my mind's eye the handmade wooden sweat lodge they used in their ceremonies. The smell of hot rocks and wood ash doused with water easily brings me back to those moments.

These reverential rituals impressed upon me feelings of a stirring awe for the mystery of it all. I was introduced to the unifying power of feminine energies expressed in and through nature, in human form. None of these experiences was cult-like or sexual in nature. I now understand that although sexual energy was present, it was held sacred. It was honored in a way that transcended the physical act—harnessing those energies in the form of the life force itself. A woman was often the focal point and at the center of many of the rituals—respected, sacred, and honored. She was Mother Earth as flesh and blood.

Chapter 2 – Life's Turning Points

In the wild dusk, resonating with the ardor of crickets and frogs, there was chanting, dancing, and ceremony acted with sacred regard, and then a final plunge into the moon-mirrored waters of the lake. The night always felt warm and rich in the lake's sweet embrace—a comforting blanket of life-filled darkness. These encounters affected and shaped me in many lasting ways, and continue to add dimension and deeper meaning to my life even now.

During those years I also passed numberless hours walking along the lake's shore and swimming in her inviting waters with snorkel and mask. I peered and dove below the clear surface into the depths of the lake, down into the dark waters with an unexplainable drive to discover something—a feeling, an essence. I didn't understand what I was searching for in words, but I had an unrelenting desire to touch something larger than and beyond myself; something intangible, persistently calling to me.

I believe I was trying to find in the waters of this beloved lake (in a child's innocent way) that immensity of awareness I tasted when my small six-year-old self expanded beyond boundaries into true limitlessness. This was the beginning of learning to love life, all of Life. I was attracted and drawn to the living vitality in Nature that was also my own vital essence. I wanted to feel in my own body and being that life force, that Spirit—in all those diverse forms and colors. I hungered to touch life's source, to uncover the deeper secrets hidden in my young heart and spirit.

What I'm much clearer about now, in relation to those childhood experiences on the lake, is that I was learning and growing in ways I could not yet understand, but that were nevertheless having a transformative effect on my life. At a subconscious, intuitive level, my comprehension of the inherent Oneness of universe had begun to germinate. Those many days spent immersed in the water or playing on the edge of the lake changed me. I became enchanted by the profusion of life everywhere: countless types of fish, frogs, insects, lizards, water birds, and a rich lively greenness all around. It was the Oneness of life in all its wondrous fecundity becoming a brightening spark inside of me. There were no toys or gadgets to distract me, just my inherent and driving curiosity. I was naturally and fully present—as children can be with such spontaneous ease.

The life-filled magic of Lake Echo and the kindness of the people who lived there helped shape my life in ways I'm only now beginning to appreciate. Those memories are a reminder and a taste of what I am learning to experience once again, but from a more expansive and unified understanding of the world. A profound wisdom entered and transformed me in those moments of wonder and silence by the lake, living among those amazing people who shared it all with me.

The Love of Wild Things

Eventually, family circumstances led me to leave Florida and travel to Colorado to live with my father and stepmother. This had a hugely important long-term influence on my life, and I still feel a real gratitude and sense of good fortune for having lived in the rural Colorado foothills during most of my teenage years and through part of college. I imagine my life would have turned out quite differently had it been otherwise.

We lived on an acre of land situated between a small foothill called a "hogback" on the front side of the house and a river bottom behind and below us. The verdant, life-filled woods, fields, and rocky hills around the river were a shared common sanctuary set aside as a natural preserve for all the houses in the neighborhood. To the west and north, there were also miles of national forest. I knew intimately and loved every inch, every nook and cranny of the landscape around our home. When I entered that wilderness, it entered me—etching in my heart and soul an ineffaceable sense of reverence and wonder. I can't imagine a better gift.

It was in this setting that an important childhood dream was able to come to fruition. Ever since the sixth grade and after reading *My Side of the Mountain* by Jean Craighead George, about a boy who lived on his own in the wilds of the Catskill Mountains, I was fascinated with the idea of living off the land and surviving in the wilderness. Learning how to hunt, fish, track, scout, build shelters, start a fire, and find wild foods became my passion. But learning those kinds of skills demanded—and this was key—a significant amount of continuous focus and attention. It required learning how to tune, sharpen, and expand my awareness so that I could become more attentive to the wisdom and endless detail of the natural world around me.

All of these skills helped me to still my mind and disengage from my thought stream much like meditation does, but naturally and without intentional effort. In other words, by learning and practicing the intricacies of tracking, searching for wild foods, and paying close attention to life's perennially changing stage, I was able to enter into a highly tuned internal silence, to enter into the moment and to begin learning and remembering our natural state of *presence*—the essence of experiences of Oneness.

These changes in how I related to the world did not happen quickly. It took several years of getting to know my wild surroundings, and it required time and attention to move beyond a surface level of relating to the world around me and to enter into a deeper relationship with myself and the natural world. I was a young teenager after all—twelve turning thirteen when we moved to the country—and my head was filled with all the typical teenage distractions and thoughts: girls, socializing, sports, freedom, and all the rest. But slowly and gratefully the wonder of Oneness that was sparked while I lived on the lake commune was reignited and began emerging anew—in an expanded, more mature way.

What changed was that I began to understand in a more comprehensive way my connection to the earth—my home. I was learning to enter into an enlivening intimacy with the natural world by learning to be present with the landscape, with life and its elements in all their amazing variety, mutability, vital richness, and interconnectedness. I was starting to get brief tastes of that Oneness; something I didn't yet understand in those terms, but it was an experience that I wanted to know better. Fortunately, I kept a journal on and off throughout those formative years; the stories I recorded helped me to revisit that metamorphosis in my life—and share this experience now.

The Teachings of a Yaqui Shaman

In tenth grade I discovered the reality- and mind-expanding books of Carlos Castaneda, and the timing couldn't have been better. His writings provided me with the direction and impetus I needed to begin to understand the possibilities of nonordinary states of consciousness and for experiencing the world in completely different and novel ways. His books, like *A Separate Reality* or *Journey to Ixtlan*, encouraged me to go further down the path initiated by the unity experiences of my childhood and inspired me to look at the mystery of the world "outside of the norm."

Carlos Castaneda, as an anthropology student working on his doctoral degree at the University of Southern California in the 1960s, claimed to have begun associating with a Yaqui shaman named Don Juan, who was living in Northern Mexico at the time. According to Castaneda, he eventually became Don Juan's apprentice. Castaneda's writings follow that relationship as it developed and changed over time.

The truth as to whether or not Castaneda actually experienced all the things he wrote about or the existence of Don Juan himself have been questioned and debated since his work was first published. In all likelihood, and I think most who have read him would agree, his books are a mix of fact and fiction. Despite the controversy, the important and frequently overlooked point is that Castaneda created an incredible story interwoven with an array of timeless wisdom and characters—all of which pointed to the very real possibility (reported by countless other shamans and spiritual seekers) of entering into new and deeper realities, or different states of conscious awareness, and of realizing our greater potentials.

Castaneda's reported apprenticeship with Don Juan initially involved the use of mind-altering and -opening peyote and psilocybin mushrooms, but overall those psychedelic substances played only a minor part in the whole story. As Castaneda made clear more than once: The use of peyote and mushrooms was a way to initially break down the barriers of belief and thought in order to open the door to the possibilities of other realities. With skilled training and time, the knowledge gained from the temporary use of these mind-expanding "helpers" was available without the need to ingest them.

As a side note: I did experiment with psychedelics on occasion while in high school and college. In fact, it was through those experimentations that it finally dawned on me what had occurred with the sugar cube. Those infrequent explorations enabled me to clearly and readily recall many of the details of that original deep taste of Oneness—details that may have remained hidden had I not tested those waters. I had come full circle in a way.

The use of hallucinogenic and mind-expanding plants, fungi, and other natural ways of altering consciousness (drums, dance, music, and deep breathing) have been pathways for opening humans to mystical and unity-type experiences in world cultures since ancient times. Our desire for experiencing transcendence and altered states of consciousness is a strong and untamable one, with deep and ancient roots. That being said, I would like to stress again that the personal unity experiences shared in the upcoming sections occurred without the use of any type of psychotropic substances.

My Universe Continues to Expand

After graduating from high school and a few years of working mindless jobs and feeling directionless, I decided to go to college. Given my growing aspiration and curiosity to learn all that I could about unity experiences, consciousness, and human possibility, it was inevitable that I would end up getting a degree in philosophy. Philosophy as a focus greatly enriched my overall college experience simply by introducing me and opening my mind to new ways of understanding and relating to the world.

I was fortunate as well to be able to explore both Western and Eastern perspectives during those five years—instead of just one side of the balance. Some of the most influential of those worldviews were Zen Buddhism, Taoism, Hinduism, Plato and the NeoPlatonists, Aristotle, Hegel, Spinoza, Kant, Whitehead, mystics like Meister Eckhart, Hildegard of Bingen, researchers of human potential and meaning like Maslow and Frankl, and others like Joseph Campbell and Alan Watts.

This wide and diverse mix of worldly wisdom, along with the structure and guidance provided by an eclectic mix of professors, enabled me to also discover the world's great Wisdom Traditions and the Perennial philosophy described earlier on in the book. It was truly a reality expander to have these amazingly rich philosophies, traditions, and perspectives floating around in my mind and sparking my imagination.

By studying in depth the Perennial philosophy and any other related knowledge I could find, I began to better understand and organize what I was learning and had already discovered about experiences of Oneness. Now I had a philosophical and psychological framework for deciphering unity experiences in a manner that made them more comprehensible and accessible. I was opened to the ideas of "flow," "peak," "mystical," and "nondual experiences," and gradually came to understand these experiences as existing along a continuum of consciousness, instead of being seen as separate, unrelated states of consciousness. Those four terms, along with several others, became a part of my growing vocabulary for conveying this spectrum of varying degrees and possibilities of Oneness. I will describe these degrees of Oneness as I have come to understand them in more detail in the next chapter.

A Jolt to My Worldview

After college I was in a quandary about what to do and where to go next. There was also that inevitable and dreaded question: What on earth are you planning on doing with a philosophy degree? I had considered the Peace Corps on several occasions, but was overwhelmed by the daunting application process. Finally I did follow through with the paperwork and was accepted—one of the best decisions of my life. My assignment was in Panama, Central America, in a place called Bocas del Toro, a chain of islands off the Caribbean coast and close to the Costa Rican border. For two years I volunteered on the main island, referred to as "Bocas Island" or "Isla Colon," teaching environmental education to the islands' kids and teachers.

Living in another country for the first time can be an incredibly powerful shock to a person's sense of normalcy, especially someone without any prior experience of living closely with entirely new and different cultures. I was only vaguely familiar with Spanish, and really had no idea how to relate to people and places so diverse and different from what I had been accustomed to. Panama is a crossroads of several different cultures, including a few major indigenous groups, so it has quite an assorted mix of customs, beliefs, and ways of being and acting in the world, ways that I had never been exposed to. As a white male who had grown up in lower middle class, mostly white America, I had a very limited and naïve view of the world.

Panama was my first experience living in a country where, in certain areas, people made do often creatively and ingeniously with very little. I resist calling it "poverty" because that's not how it felt; it was just a much simpler life, with fewer "things." This exposure to people who lived, often happily, with so much less than I was used to shook my worldview to its very roots. It opened me to larger possibilities and it pushed my limited perspective to expand.

I call these sorts of experiences that make it possible to at least temporarily free ourselves from rigid beliefs and attitudes and to open our minds to bigger picture possibilities "jolts." Travel, in general, if done in a way that encourages real contact and connection with locals, is an excellent example of a jolt. Living in new places is often enough to rattle one's comfort zone and begin to break down the confining walls that we create around ourselves.

In Panama I also was able to renew my relationship with the ocean, and I was introduced to the intricate web and wilds of the rainforest. The islands of Bocas del Toro are a unique place in that the pristine ecosystems of ocean and rainforest coexist right next to one another, creating an incredibly stirring and inspiring physical, sensory, and emotional contrast. And it was in this setting of rainforest and ocean where some of my more profound unity experiences unfolded.

One of the Herd and Back to Panama

What to do next with my life? Despite the many transformative experiences and important growth as a volunteer in the Peace Corps, I still craved all the proverbial carrots at the end of the stick: relationships, a good job, money, a house, self-improvement, "cool" experiences, comfort, entertainment, adventure, and travel. It was that well-trodden, ego-driven path of searching hopefully (yet fruitlessly) for true and lasting happiness in the external world of things, money, accomplishments, and the insatiable desire for more.

Over and over, I sought that ever-elusive, perfect situation and life. And even though, at an intuitive level, I knew there would be no end to running after this mirage, I had to go through it, live it; I had to experience firsthand the unavoidable and sometimes intense ups and downs of a life caught in the web of an ego-dominated, self-centered mindset.

Throughout those years of chasing after worldly fulfillment and happiness, I did continue with various meditation practices, as well as reading about and exploring in more depth the possibilities of unity experiences, spirituality, and human potential. But progress and motivation waxed and waned depending on the changing circumstances of my life. I had learned a lot, or at least thought I had, on the path of understanding, but the limitations and frustration created by my willing yet mindless participation in becoming one of the herd started weighing me down. I desperately needed a consistent and dependable means of rooting out the habitual junk, the fear, the conditioning, the self-absorption, and the ego-imposed limitations to further realization and discovery.

Finally, after a major low point in my life—a job I hated, an unresolved end to some important relationships, along with a heavy and dark depression that was slowly sinking its claws into me—I acted on a long and deeply held calling to write. I became inspired to give substance, clarity, and order to the transformative life experiences I talk about in this book. I wanted more than anything else to put these important insights and revelations into a form that would hopefully help me, and eventually others, to recognize and follow in a clear and simple way the wisdom of Oneness we all hunger for at some level in our lives. So I dropped everything, trusted, and jumped.

It was that leap that led me back to the wilds of Bocas del Toro, Panama—almost two decades after the Peace Corps. I knew that by living in Bocas town again I would be able to greatly simplify my life, giving me the time, space, and freedom to begin the process of clearly creating a foundation for *The Possibilities of Oneness*. The knowledge, the wisdom, and stories were all inside me, but they were nascent, spread out and not in a form that I could write about yet.

    I had been traveling to and sometimes living in Panama for short periods of time since leaving the Peace Corps, but this occasion was very different. This time there was an inspired vision calling to finally become real and tangible. I had come full circle again—one circle among a spiral of many.

Chapter 3
Degrees of Oneness

What I began to recognize in college while delving into and studying Eastern and Western philosophies, along with the world's Wisdom Traditions, is that unity experiences can be loosely arranged and understood along a simple spectrum of expanding states of consciousness based on lesser and greater degrees of experienced Oneness or wholeness. On one end of this spectrum there is a seemingly undeniable separateness from the world, while at the other end there is the experience of complete and expansive Oneness with all that exists and arises moment to moment. And then there are all the possible variations and degrees of experienced Oneness in between.

I eventually came up with a simplified way of picturing and talking about this spectrum of expanding levels of consciousness and Oneness. But instead of using a linear model for depicting these openings in consciousness, I decided it made more sense to use a series of expanding, concentric circles. The accompanying diagram demonstrates this continuum of experience using those terms that for me point to progressively increasing and inclusive states of awareness and Oneness: *ego, flow, wonder, high peak,* and *nondual* states.

As illustrated in this series of concentric circles, ego is the smallest circle; the most confined and limited state of consciousness. Each successive circle moving outward represents a transition into increasing degrees of awareness and experienced Oneness. As one moves outward, the hold of ego lessens while our experience of wholeness, connectedness, and presence begin to widen and become more inclusive.

In other words, the expanding levels of consciousness are *ego*—the most contracted and limited state of awareness, moving outward into the *flow state,* expanding next into what I refer to as the *wonder state,* opening further still into *mystical or high peak states,* and finally into *nondual states*—cosmic or total unitive consciousness—the infinity outside of the circle and the foundation of the circle itself.

The Ego State—A Separate Self

What I have come to realize from my own experience and from the lived wisdom of others is that there is an inverse relationship between an ego-centered, self-absorbed life and the capacity we have to shift into more unifying states of awareness. Put simply, as the grip of ego increases, our inherent ability to wake up to the possibilities of Oneness decreases. The more we live and act from within a self-restricted consciousness with its conditioned patterns of thinking and acting, with its rigid concepts, fixed ideas, and beliefs, the more unlikely it will be for us to rediscover our far richer and natural state of consciousness—presence. Without presence, we no longer know how to be fully in the moment and to disentangle from a constant preoccupation with a past and a future that exist only in our minds—all of which are the critical first steps for waking up to Oneness.

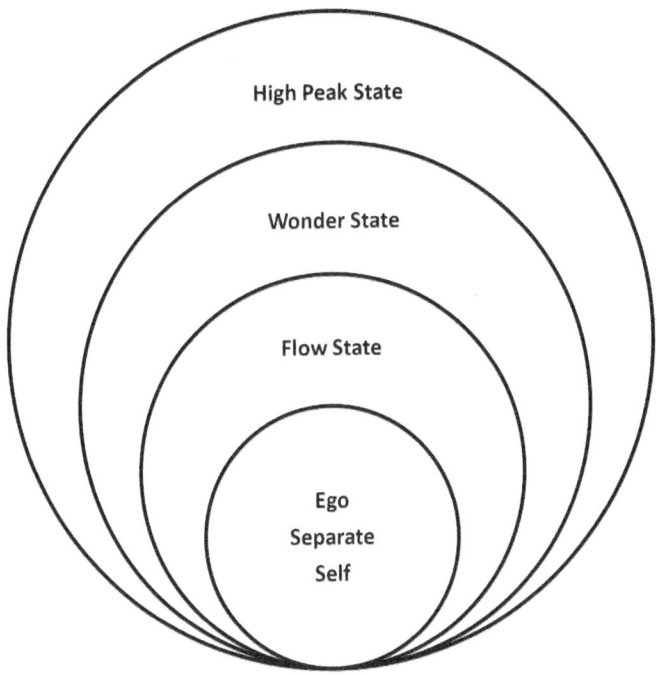

Moreover, as our learned sense of being a self separate from the world around us grows, the boundaries of ego become increasingly solid and inflexible; the distinctness of subject and object, outside and inside seems to be unquestionable. We end up living mostly in our heads with a never-ending stream of thoughts that help to sustain this mentally fabricated belief in a separate self. And it is a self that often lives in fear and needs to be constantly defended, that wants more and more security, sensations, and control. Like the clouded waves of the ocean and wave metaphor, awareness becomes progressively blinded and cut off from its Source and deeper wisdom.

Ego consciousness as our center and dominant mode of awareness allows us to experience only a small fraction of what is possible. If we are not taught to loosen and expand the ego's boundaries, to see beyond its narrowly constructed walls and through the cloud it forms, it begins to create a gravitational pull on consciousness that keeps awareness mired in a greatly diminished and limited state. This ego-based sense of separation is a necessary first step in our development as humans, but if it is not outgrown it can become a stunted and extremely divisive form of consciousness.

What is crucial to remember though is that ego consciousness is only *one way* of seeing and interpreting this universe and the infinite ocean of being, awareness, and energy that is our matrix of existence. It is not the only way, but we forget that. One of our greatest powers as conscious beings is that we can purposefully direct our awareness through attention and intention to grow beyond its own "self"-created limitations. We have the power and choice to change.

The Flow State

Moving from ego at center, outward into the next circle of awareness, we find flow experiences. According to Mihaly Csikszentmihalyi (author of *Flow—The Psychology of Optimal Experience*), the "flow experience," or "getting into the zone," is a temporary state brought about by an intrinsically meaningful and rewarding activity that engages one's attention, focus, and concentration to the fullest degree by challenging the limit or edge of one's skills and abilities. It is typically an activity that is goal or rule oriented, providing increasing levels of clear feedback, which allows for further improvement and escalating degrees of challenge. From my own experience, flow can also happen during activities that are not necessarily goal centered or overly challenging, but that nevertheless still require a certain amount of directed focus—like mindful walks, running, or easy, flowing hikes or bike rides.

How then does the flow state relate to experiences of Oneness? During flow experiences there is a "self-forgetting" immersion in an activity we enjoy, an intense focusing of attention on an action that is challenging in some way and that requires us to stop overthinking. Once the mind noise begins to fade, a spontaneous falling away of our habitual feeling of being separate from the world around us begins. While flow experiences are occurring, self-awareness will often start to merge with the action at hand; they become one, a unified flow. This is a key and crucial point; it is, I believe, the heart of what makes flow and unity experiences in general so gratifying and fulfilling. To let go of that incessant self-concept and mental chatter, the ego and all its accompanying preoccupations, even for a short time, can be immensely liberating and some of our happiest moments in life.

The types of activities that might help one enter into a state of flow are diverse and wide-ranging. Some require more physical involvement and the need to acquire a certain level of skill. These might include, among many others, sports such as skiing, snowboarding, rock climbing, kayaking/rafting, surfing, scuba diving, mountain or road biking, motocross, or car racing.

Other activities for entering the flow state that normally involve less risk might include art, dance, martial arts, meditation, writing, gardening, hiking, walking, golfing, tennis, snorkeling, listening to and playing music, watching a movie, cooking, entertaining, games, or engaging conversation. These are only a few of the possibilities. Some of the unity experiences I describe next include several of the above doorways to flow.

It is not so much the specific activity itself that matters as the person's attitude, motivation, and state of mind-body going into the experience. Flow does require a certain amount of skillful know-how developed through experience and practice, until after a while, one's actions become a kind of effortless effort—without thought, natural, and spontaneous. Yet flow is definitely not about going into an "autopilot" mode or "spacing out"; it is the opposite, in fact. To re-emphasize, flow requires a high degree of concentrated yet expanded attention, a stilled mind with very few intervening thoughts; in other words, *flow demands presence.*

The flow state is the beginning of loosening the boundaries of the self and temporarily rising above and getting outside that contracted state of self-consciousness produced and sustained by the thinking mind. It's about those precious moments of momentarily forgetting and transcending our stubborn self-concept by learning to unite awareness with whatever we are doing in the moment through greater presence. With flow experiences in particular, our sense of self may still be very close at hand, along with intermittent thoughts, but with flow an integrative expansion of awareness has begun. It can be a starting point for waking up to a more unified state of consciousness and for regaining a spontaneity that is often lost in modern life.

The Wonder State

The next circle outward is what I refer to as the "wonder state"—a term I coined to describe unity-type experiences I was having that were similar in some ways to flow experiences, but at the same time went beyond them. I wanted a way of categorizing experiences that felt different from and more expansive than flow, but still did not possess the degree or the depth of Oneness experienced during deeper unity or higher peak experiences.

Although there are parallels between the flow experience and the wonder state, there are also important differences. Unlike flow, the wonder state does not require any particular skills, rules, goals, or challenges to enter it. It actually arises out of the opposite of those things. Instead of having attention focused on action and on doing, the wonder state is about opening to what is, to just being. It too is an expanded yet focused state, but the wonder state is more receptive in nature and entails moving into a state of awareness where one is able to let go, let be, and let happen; it is about simply being—in wonder.

The wonder state is similar to meditative mind or mindfulness as described in Buddhism. It is that paradoxical state when conscious awareness has become focused and concentrated, while simultaneously being expansive and panoramic—what I prefer to call "awarefulness" or "nowfulness." They are both words with a similar intended meaning as the Buddhist term "mindfulness," but mindfulness for me sounds too much like being "full of mind activity—thought," which is exactly the state of mind we want to be able to disengage from.

One of the primary goals of meditation is to learn to still the mind, to become present, and wake up to a sense of groundedness and expansiveness that reconnects us with the bigger picture of Life. It is a pathway for moving from small-minded awareness to big-minded awareness. Practicing meditation, even though it has been sporadic for me at times, gradually enabled me to discover the wonder state—the developed, adult version of what is often natural for children if they are encouraged to explore their innate curiosity and imagination. Through meditation I learned to intentionally and consistently return to the Now, which is all there is, and to be totally present and attentively tuned to whatever was unfolding in the moment.

During shifts into the wonder state, I am also able to more clearly and easily perceive the interconnectedness of the natural world and the One Energy that underlies all life. As thoughts still and quietness settles in, there is a gradual opening into a penetrating sense of awareness that is deep and wide, rooted and revealing, all at once. In those moments I look out into the world and see its living vitality and wholeness shine through. It's a strange sight and feeling at first, but it is a truly mind-blowing experience when this shift happens. The world suddenly becomes indescribably vibrant and alive—*all of it.*

As the wonder state deepens, there is a growing certainty that the universe is an ocean of infinite energy and awareness with innumerable possibilities. And in that feeling there is an upwelling of enlivening joy and gratitude. All is perfect and utterly beautiful as it is—with nothing added, nothing projected, and nothing needed.

The wonder state often occurs spontaneously, given the right circumstances; for example, those sudden heart-opening, mind-stopping moments of beauty, power, and astonishment experienced when seeing a place like the Grand Canyon or one of the other natural "wonders" of our world for the first time.

It can be found as well when an exalted sense of connection and Oneness overtakes us as we experience unconditional love for another person—family, friend, or stranger. It might be the amazed wonder of a child being born, or when the world is allowed to be as it is without thoughts of labeling it or changing it in some way, when it is simply experienced for the miraculous wonder that it is—direct and without judgment or desire that it be different.

It never ceases to amaze me—the dramatic yet subtle shift that occurs when moving into the wonder state. In a simple way, it is like finally, and for the first time, being able to see the three-dimensional image hidden within the two-dimensional pictures of the popular *Magic Eye* books. That shift also requires a stilling of the mind, focus, and attention to open us to a normally unseen dimension and deeper reality.

High Peak Experiences

The outermost circle of circles represents high peak or mystical experiences. Unfortunately, the term "mystical" tends to carry a history of negative associations and misunderstanding. The word is often erroneously viewed as expressing a strictly religious experience available only to a special and select few, or it is misinterpreted as woo-woo, magical, and esoteric in a way that makes it seem beyond the reach or interest of most. In reality, we all have a natural aptitude for mystical experience, although this potential is rarely encouraged.

Because of the burden of baggage placed on the mystical, I prefer to use the term "high peak" for describing those deeper, more expansive unity experiences that allow one to move beyond and outside our normal day-to-day state of consciousness. The degree of Oneness experienced during high peak experiences is a shift into an even fuller sense of union with some facet of the world, with nature, with the cosmos, or with the Infinity we call Spirit, God, Life, or Mystery—or however one prefers to relate to Ultimate Reality.

Peak experiences in general (coined by Abraham Maslow in the 1960s to describe this state) are those precious, unforgettable moments in our lives when we glimpse the greater inherent human potentials and possibilities that are open to us. They are those experiences that are at once our highest fulfillment and our deepest joy and happiness, powerful experiences of self-transcendence, of Oneness, of love—of recognizing our ultimate identity with the greater source of our existence. Peak experiences open our minds and lives to new, more expansive, and optimal ways of being and living. I use the term high peak to point to those experiences that are the "highest" expression of these kinds of peak possibilities.

During high peak experiences, the ego is transcended and its limiting boundaries almost completely dissolve. The perceived duality between subject and object, self and the world, temporarily vanishes, leaving a profound Oneness with all that is in its place. Inside and outside, the experiencer and the experienced, the seer and the seen, the lover and the loved become one. All that remains is pure experience right here and right now—presence. The "I" falls away and there is an awakening to the all that is one and the one that is all, to the pure awareness that we are before the thinking mind begins to filter, judge, and shape our experience. Or to return to the ocean-wave metaphor, the clouded wave clears and becomes transparent, finally recognizes the truth of its inseparability from the boundless, timeless ocean of Oneness.

Cosmic Consciousness—Total Unitive Consciousness

Cosmic consciousness, or absolute nondual Oneness, is the inconceivable infinity that surrounds and is the ground of all the other circles. To experience this reawakening of consciousness to what we are in essence is a realization of one of our greatest of human potentials. In a state of total unitive consciousness, the other circles in the diagram that represent increasing levels of unified awareness disappear. This is what I experienced when I ate the sugar cube as a kid, the cosmic consciousness or nondual Oneness I described earlier in the "meanings of Oneness."

Even the most intense and profound high peak experiences will still retain some trace of self-identity, even if faint or unfelt. The reason for that is that unity experiences—flow, wonder, and high peak states remain relative and conditional in the sense of still maintaining a certain level of duality, of subject-object awareness, however minute. Whereas cosmic, nondual consciousness is the whole shebang; self is completely transcended and falls away with no trace. I and universe become one; all boundaries, all distinctiveness, all separateness dissolve. The wave experiences its Oneness with Ocean in the deepest, fullest way possible, knows that it was never separate.

True and full nondual experiences are still relatively rare, I believe, at this stage in our journey as a species. But the potential is always there. Some level of consistent unity or integrative consciousness might very well be the base consciousness for future generations. It is a beautiful hope and vision to contemplate.

What Unity Experiences Share and What They Are Not

Something to keep in mind when reading through the upcoming experiences of Oneness is that although these kinds of experiences can differ in terms of when, where, and how they happen, they also share certain important elements or feelings in common: a return to the power of presence and a diminishment or falling away of feeling like a separate, isolated self; a vibrant and energized aliveness; a changed perception of the flow of time and the limitations of space; a sense of wide-open freedom and limitlessness; an unshakeable sense that all is well; deep feelings of higher love, gratitude, wonder, and mystery; knowing without doubt feelings of connectedness, meaning, and oneness—and more. This is not to say that all unity experiences will have these same characteristics every time. That too will vary depending on the nature of the particular experience.

Given the parallels and similarities that unity experiences often share, it is also important to be aware that those common elements as described above have been unavoidably broken up and laid out into parts, into mental- and language-based divisions. When in truth, as experiences of Oneness are actually taking place, they happen as a continuous and fluid whole. All of these possible and separate experiences are in reality unfolding as "one" experience, as a single thought-transcending event, some more intensely than others depending on the depth of the experience. It is similar to how a river is composed of different depths, faster and slower currents, varied levels of clarity, but it is still the same river—unified and whole.

As is apparent by now, I believe experiences of Oneness are some of the most genuinely fulfilling, transformative, and joyful experiences possible for human beings. They are glimpses and tastes of a type of integrative consciousness that speaks of one of our most important and fulfilling human potentials. The way I see it, how could we not want these possibilities of higher consciousness to be the rule instead of the exception, our base and center rather than the rare occurrence? The beauty is that these experiences are within reach if we choose to stretch and open our minds even a little.

In light of the different ways experiences of Oneness are similar, it is also helpful to note what experiences of Oneness are *not*, or how they might be misinterpreted or misunderstood. First, unity experiences are not some kind of super mental power or a sudden all-pervading intellectual or factual knowing of everything at once, apprehending all there is to know in the universe instantly and completely. Unity experiences as they are happening have nothing to do with the comprehension of facts, information, rational thought processes, or the intellect. This kind of conceptual activity may be in the background, but it is silenced and only brought to the foreground later when attempting to describe the experience.

Further, during unity experiences, the physical body remains solid and stable; it doesn't disappear or break down or actually physically merge with what is around it, although it may feel that way at times. Important to remember as well is that experiences of Oneness are much different from simply daydreaming or performing an action like a robot or in a way that is trancelike, mindless, or habitual. Awareness and attention are actually often diminished in those situations and they are quite different from the aliveness and vibrant awareness experienced during unity experiences.

All that I have written so far has been a way to set the stage for the remaining sections of the book—the lived experiences of Oneness and the Thirteen Circles of Timeless Wisdom.

Chapter 4
Experiences of Oneness from My Life

In the upcoming chapters, I share a wide-ranging selection of stories describing in detail several of the transformative unity experiences that I have had over the years. Some of these openings to Oneness arose as sudden illuminations—flashes of knowing that occurred spontaneously and unexpectedly. At other times, they were measured and gradually unfolding experiences discovered with directed purpose to remember and regain presence in my day-to-day life. My intention in sharing these particular experiences of Oneness is to provide a broad enough variety that most everyone will be able to connect at some level with similar experiences they themselves have had—or have at least heard or read about.

Because it is such an important point, I want to reiterate that what is experienced during unity moments is for the most part a directly felt and raw experience; it is not mediated or filtered by thought, and is free from the usual conceptual projections, judgments, or expectations that might interfere with and distort the experience. They are those moments when the wave clears and awareness opens to a bigger world, a larger ocean of Oneness and wonder rarely tasted. So in telling these stories (many drawn from years of journal writings), I tried to recapture those initial impressions as purely as possible, without changing the originality of the experience.

Language, of course, cannot fully convey the original wholeness and flow of unity experiences. It can only point to the experience after the fact, break it down, and express it in parts, as mental abstractions. But that is both the gift and challenge of human consciousness and memory: Self-awareness makes it possible to be conscious of Oneness in the first place, but it's extremely difficult to adequately describe this knowingness in words. My hope is that despite the limitations of words to recapture my original experience, at some level, the "feeling" of Oneness will be transmitted to you through my storytelling.

Also, although we can encourage and, through some form of consistent meditative or "presence practice," prepare the ground for unity experiences to happen, they are fundamentally uncontrollable and beyond being forced. The more "I" want them to happen, the less likely they are to occur. It is only when we begin to move beyond the personal sense of an "I" and disengage from our habitual need to try to control and manipulate reality that the possibilities of these unified states of consciousness become more likely.

The bottom line is this: Unity experiences cannot be sought after like any other self-centered accomplishment or good feeling. Experiences of Oneness will remain out of reach if chased after to impress, to outdo, or if pursued in order to reach some ecstatic high. Ego-centered, emotionally charged motives like these only make the deeper unity experience more elusive and unlikely to occur. And I do speak from experience on this point.

Flow, wonder, high peak, or cosmic shifts in consciousness can be momentous, mind- and life-changing events, but care must be taken to avoid the possibility of turning the desire for more such experiences into a "search" or an "achievement"—or even an addiction

CHAPTER 4–EXPERIENCES OF ONENESS FROM MY LIFE

of sorts. To do so is a contradiction and a misunderstanding of what these experiences really are and what they mean. Unity experiences are simply glimpses into the cleared and transparent waters of who we are in truth and essence, into the pure awareness that is already and always our truest state of being.

Finally, experiences of Oneness often involve a natural movement and transitioning between the differing levels and depths as I have described them—depending on how much of a sense of ego is present in the experience. For instance, the more active flow state will frequently transition into the less active and more receptive wonder state, and vice versa. The wonder state can go deeper and expand into a higher peak or mystical experience. Or a higher peak experience can contract somewhat and shift to the wonder or flow state.

With nondual experiences, or complete unitive consciousness, on the other hand, the sense of time, self, and sequence are suspended. All that remains is pure conscious awareness. The only shift left at that point is back into some degree of separative consciousness, but often with a more unitive foundation now in place.

On to the stories then.

Part One
One with the Living Ocean

A Second Taste

My first clear reconnection with Oneness happened while I was swimming in the ocean ten years after my original childhood experience. I was in the tenth grade, visiting my grandparents who lived on the Atlantic coast of Florida. Since those early years living on Lake Echo, water had the power to stir deep feelings of mystery and wonder in me, so it was fitting that this reawakening to Oneness took place while I was playing in the warm, turquoise waters and waves of the Atlantic Ocean.

I had been swimming alone close to shore for an hour or so, diving and surfacing in a dolphin-like motion, in rhythm with the glassy incoming waves. The sun had set behind me, yet the endless eastern horizon in front of me was illuminated with embers of the sun's remaining radiance. The light from the descending sun lent a strange beauty and golden glow to the darkening sky's rich blues and grays.

My undulating, rhythmic movements were in the spirit of play and a simple expression of the tremendous happiness I felt moving light and free through the warm embrace of the ocean. There was nothing intentional or planned about my play. I continued this sinuous rhythm of diving and surfacing unaware of time. When I dove downward and moved forward underwater, I would release a great exhalation of bubbles that would wrap themselves sensuously around my body; the sound and feeling were mesmerizing. As I rose out of the water, pushing myself off the sandy bottom, I would take in a big breath before diving down again, timing my dive to enter the shimmering face of a wave right before it crested.

I realize now that because of the rhythmic, mind-stilling movements I was making (like the whirling dervish dances of the Sufi mystics), my attention was diverted from its usual thinking mode, allowing me to become fully absorbed in the movement of breath, body, and water. It was a spontaneous moving meditation that enabled my thinking mind to quiet naturally. Awareness felt focused on the moment, yet wide and open. All my senses became sharper and more perceptive.

And to clarify, I didn't jump into the ocean and start diving up and down with the intention of emptying my mind of all thoughts; in fact, I remember having two thoughts in particular in the beginning: either this up and down thing is going to attract a shark or someone is going to think I'm drowning. In other words, I wasn't expecting to create some kind of extraordinary experience. Instead, I was simply letting things happen and returning naturally and intuitively to presence. I wasn't trying to control the experience, so my thoughts dropped off quickly and I was then able to return easily and fully to the present moment—to the richness and possibilities of play in the Now.

I knew and felt with such vividness the ancient salty smell and taste of the sea, the sound of splashing and crashing waves, the bubbles and breathing, the distant lonely calls of seagulls, and glimpses of endless sky and ocean gradually darkening, transforming as one. It was a single unified perception without thought and happening all at once.

What stands out most clearly though, similar to what I experienced as a child but not quite as intense or as full, is that feeling of starting to lose and let go of my habitual sense of self. Those I/me/my boundaries began to soften, to melt away and become transparent to the deeper undercurrents of wholeness and connectivity beneath. With the growing silence of my mind, awareness began to open, to move outward, outside of my head and into a bigger kind of awareness. I remember suddenly feeling and being overtaken by such an immense joyfulness and lightness of being. I felt the deepest love and gratitude for being alive at that moment. It was love without thought or condition. It was big love and it overtook me.

I stopped moving and simply stood there up to my chest in the mellowing ocean waters, feeling my heart open and flow into the infinite horizon—into the mystery. My body, awareness, and being suddenly remembered its Oneness with ocean, sky, and the beyond; "my" body became "no" body and returned to the presence underneath my thinking mind: pure awareness. All that remained was a profound feeling of belonging and an intimate, inseparable connection to everything.

I was momentarily freed from my usual identification with a personality, with places, things, people, or the doings of the world. I had realized an unexpected, enlightening liberation from the pull of ego—temporarily at least. And that is by far one of the most vitalizing and unforgettable feelings in the world.

This experience was a long time coming. I believe that the seed planted in me as a child of six was in much need of a little water and light. And that's what it received. This was a major turning point, in the sense that it sparked the rediscovery of the power of unity experiences from a more mature perspective. It reignited in me the desire to intentionally explore the deeper meaning and potentiality of these experiences. I now recognized in a more conscious way my deep-rooted hunger for the unknown, the desire to know and understand the essence and truth of the world beyond appearances, beyond conditioning—the truth of self and of Life.

As the doors gradually opened, I began to see that there were more ways than one for interpreting reality; this was a giant step in terms of opening my mind to the possibilities and power of awareness, perception, and attention.

The Big Island

A few years after finishing my service in the Peace Corps, around 1999, I lived on the Big Island of Hawaii for a year. The islands are undeniably enchanting and affecting in a palpable and powerful way. And for me, the Big Island is especially like that. While I lived there, I worked in the evenings as a waiter and explored during the day. I lived simply and made decent money, so that gave me abundant time to get out and learn about and experience the island up close and personal. Some of the experiences told here date from that time, most of them involving the ocean, of course.

Humpback Wonder

It was a brilliant sunny day in a harbor close to where I worked. The ocean was gleaming with sparkling whites and deep sapphire blues, like living rays of light rising with some unknown purpose from the mysterious and unseen depths. I was with a longtime friend, each of us in a kayak, paddling the bay and hoping for an encounter with a humpback whale. On several previous occasions, we had seen and heard their enormous spouts blasting off in the distance, but we were never close enough to see the actual whales. We would paddle intently toward the general vicinity of the last spout, eager for at least a glimpse of one of the magnificent giants, but invariably they would seem to magically disappear and reappear off in the distance—surprisingly elusive for such behemoths.

After being out on the water for a few hours, we decided to call it a day and started paddling toward shore. It was then, of course, that the whale appeared and not in the distance but right next to our kayaks. I'd never seen a whale up close. It was a life changer to say the least.

All of the sudden I saw and felt a billowing surge of sea water next to and below my kayak, then a small swirl, followed by a huge upwelling. I knew immediately what was happening—or hoped I did. I filled with an intense excitement and anticipation; I felt no real fear or panic or any genuine sense of impending danger, only a riveting and beautiful uncertainty. My friend was still paddling close by but backed off a bit—just in case. I could feel it in my whole body as this massive dark form moved slowly on all sides and underneath the kayak, lifting it gently upward.

I became charged with an intense focus and immediacy, yet there was something opening up in me at the same time. The inexplicable feeling of time stopping and space becoming less defined took over. I felt a vibratory electrical presence—rising in the water, in the air, and in me—taking hold and shaking my world.

Then the whale seemed to disappear into the depths as quickly as it had appeared, but it left in its wake a reverberating silence, alive and brimming with power. I knew it wasn't over and the whale soon returned, its curiosity not quite placated, I guess.

It is strange to see an amorphous living body so immense that there's no way of defining its shape or size. But that soon changed. Out of the ocean's rippling blues, filled with the whale's moving dark grays, there suddenly appeared a colossal eye. Right there beside me! I could have reached out and touched it. It was a deep, dark, brownish black, the size of a dinner plate, bottomless yet radiant and aware, shining with undeniable intelligence and the fire of life.

The whale was peering at me with such obvious curiosity. In that eye was everything. It was a glimpse into the Source itself and into the endless creative genius of the universe embodied as the enormous form of a whale. It looked at and into me in its slow and inquisitive way and allowed me the privilege of being close to it without fear. I was held in complete, silenced amazement and wonderment. Here was the essence and wonder of Life, worldly and infinite, right before me.

The pure exhilaration of the humpback's powerful and giant presence was mind blowing—literally mind stopping. The habitual sense of being a self distinct from the world around me eased up, and I was shocked fully into the Now. My mind's usual mode of thinking and projecting onto the world my ideas of how things should or shouldn't be was overwhelmed into stillness and intense presence instead. In that moment, the ego-perpetuated and thought-generated boundary between "self" and "whale" began to dissolve and become transparent to the underlying unity that connects all life and everything. Time, space, and self were temporarily transcended, and I experienced a waking up to the Oneness that is our shared home.

My heart began overflowing with a deep reverence for this giant living being; I felt an overpowering pressure on my chest that opened outward and poured into the ocean and sky. Such moments, as everyone knows at some level, are among the most beautiful and profound experiences we can have in life; they transform us.

The Sacred Valley

On the Big Island there is a valley called Waipio. It is a breathtaking and stunning wildness that is held sacred by the Hawaiian people, present and past. You can feel its power in the life, the air, the earth, and the water that form and shape it; this potent life force or living vitality ("mana" as it is sometimes called by Hawaiians) shines through everywhere and is easily sensed. Waipio is one of those special places on our planet that naturally evokes strong feelings of reverence, respect, and sacredness.

That being said, the valley can be a busy place at times. On this particular morning though, I had the river-rock and sand-bottomed surf break all to myself. The ocean shone with steely blue grays, clear, and glassy, and an ascending sun was slowly rising into a depthless cerulean sky. Rays of sunlight danced a strange enchantment—lighting the world both outwardly and from within. At both ends of the deep valley, waterfalls cascaded down vertical walls, tumbling wildly, their spray creating a spectrum of circular rainbow hues. The awesomeness of the moment easily moved me into silenced wonder—*the wonder state.*

The ancient salt and life, the smell of the ocean, the cool touch of seawater, the spirit-lifting sensations of waves, birds, tropical greens, and waterfalls all joined with a multitude of other colors, forms, and feelings, merging into one.

Suddenly a mother humpback whale and her calf surfaced about fifty meters away from where I was floating on my surfboard. Could this really be happening? It was a gift beyond belief. As I watched the whales, that familiar feeling of intense connection and overflowing gratitude filled me—pushing out thoughts, allowing an overwhelming love for life to pour forth. The elation that shot through me at that moment was indescribable; I couldn't contain the sheer exultation of it all. I remember bursting into tears and soulful laughter at the same time, and how that surprised and delighted me. The whales, ocean, sky, and earth felt to be inseparable with my body and being.

So overtaken by the immense and powerful beauty of the experience, my mind stilled deeply. Again, there was that inexpressible feeling of transcending time, of moving beyond temporal and spatial boundaries. Space and time seem to transform into an indivisible whole—that is, the normal sense of separateness melts away; the moment becomes timeless and the defining qualities of space less certain.

Floating in the ocean that day, with the whales and in the middle of a sacred Hawaiian valley, a feeling of unbounded energy and of unlimited possibilities permeated my being, but the "my" fell away.

Presence returned, became primary and self-identity momentarily dissolved into the surrounding sea of life, energy, and awareness. Consciousness unfurled and expanded beyond its usual contracted boundaries like a sail opening to an infinite wind.

A Circle of Rays

Water, as we know well, is one of the primary and elemental sources of life; it is the essence of the blood that bathes, supports, and brings life to every cell of our bodies. Playing in this miraculous, liquid medium has always fascinated and drawn me. It is one of the ultimate places to revel in the wonders of our planet. It is that rare space where the constant pull of earth's gravity can be eased temporarily, where the sense of an enveloping weightlessness and a hypnotic slow-motion flight is made possible. Swimming in and above water is truly like a flowing, liquid flight. To me, being embraced by water can feel like losing the defining lines of skin and body—and finding some long-forgotten freedom.

And in the ocean especially, underneath its mercury-like silver surface, new worlds and countless life forms and relationships are astoundingly revealed, and all of them are attention-focusing and awareness-opening revelations of form and space.

While living in Hawaii, I heard about a manta ray dive or snorkel trip being offered by some of the local dive shops. I mistakenly assumed it would be super expensive so I never looked into it. But on a return visit, I discovered that the cost of the snorkel trip was actually reasonable. I decided to give it a try.

Off the Kona coast in a certain place and during specific times of the year, there are large gatherings of manta rays that congregate to feed. What attracts them are dense populations of zooplankton—the manta ray's primary food source. To help draw in even greater concentrations of these tiny animals, a circle of bright dive lights is set up on the ocean floor right around dusk, about eight meters below the surface. The beaming lights begin magnetizing myriad microscopic ocean creatures, which, in turn, attract the hungry rays. They feed with their huge, vacuous mouths wide open, sifting and sieving the barely visible shimmering plankton as they soar in vertical circles through the theater of light.

When I entered into that incredible scene for the first time, it blew away my mind stream of commentary and my usual sense of self and separateness almost instantly. Instead, I was inundated with an otherworldly feeling of living beauty and greater possibilities. Then there was the wondrous privilege of being in the water with the mantas themselves, to actually be able to fly circles with these soaring marvels of the ocean. It was truly extraordinary. And although the manta rays were obviously aware of me and the many other people nearby, they appeared unbothered by it, intent on filling their bellies.

To enter this dreamlike stage of light and motion below me, I would take a massive breath and dive down with only snorkel, mask, fins, and a weight belt. As I swam downward into the light, surrounded by walls of watery darkness, thoughts disappeared and were replaced with an uplifting and uncontainable rush of excitement. I attempted to shift the energy of my body and mind in a way that allowed me to synchronize with the mantas' perfect motion, our bodies not touching but close. I swam slow-motion circles with these winged giants, flesh and flowing blood so similar to my own within arm's reach.

As I swam, I began to feel like there was a merging of life energies and awareness. That feeling, as with the whale, was charged—resonant and electric. The usual feeling of being separated from everything around me diminished, the push and pull of the constant internal dialogue filling my head lessened. My mind stilled and there was a disengagement from thinking about what I was doing. I had returned to being present, to presence. And in that presence I was able to enter into a deeper connectedness with all that surrounded me. It was an opening of consciousness that began to include the manta rays in a way that joined us, made our distinctness and individuality seem less solid, less sure. To fully convey that astonishing sense of knowing another living being as both distinct yet inseparable from my own seems impossible.

The hours I spent with these graceful sea creatures, not surprisingly, felt like minutes. Their bodies became my body; their flowing movements, my movement. Thoughts arose at times, but they seemed distant, ephemeral, and mostly practical in nature. The little thinking that did occur came and went; I was outside of it, watching, letting it come and letting it go. As the boundaries of self continued to open, "I" intermittently disappeared into all that was arising in the moment. The perfect form and fluid circles of the mantas, the surreal, revealing power of the lights, being suspended and weightless in water, the other divers, my body, and the growing feeling of becoming selfless all merged into one unified awareness.

I relish this memory of being so close and connected to another living being, a creature of the ocean expressed in perfect serpentine curves and so alive with the creative energy of life.

Dolphins—Spinner's Play

The obvious intelligence of dolphins as well as their unbelievable fluidity, agility, and the compelling strength of their physical movements are widely known. Maybe those impressions about dolphins come from having watched documentaries about them, from having seen their undeniable curiosity and playful antics from a boat, or perhaps even from swimming with captive dolphins. Much can be learned about them in these ways. On the other hand, it is a completely different story when you experience dolphins in the wild, in the water, and when they are free to choose whether or not to interact with you.

While exploring on the Big Island, I discovered a small hidden bay that I had missed during previous searches in the area. In the center of this bay is a blue hole that shimmers with a dance of depthless, translucent azures and emerald greens. I was out snorkeling early in the day with the hope of seeing the green sea turtles that often frequent protected bays like this one. I didn't know the bay very well and had slowly wandered out to a place where the coral ended and the sea bottom seemed to drop off into invisible glimmering depths, which, as my eyes adjusted, turned out to be a white sandy bottom many meters down.

Despite the drop-off, I continued to explore, enjoying the fascinating sensation of hovering over what felt like a bottomless abyss. The sensation was bizarre; the lack of depth perception or any real sense of direction made the experience alien, mesmerizing me to the extent that it seemed at times like I was shifting into pure, disembodied awareness.

Then, out of that deep blue void, I detected motion. In the distance, grayish apparitions appeared and moved in my direction. The sight struck me with fear at first. But soon enough, I could see that it was a group of dolphins swimming toward me—Hawaiian spinner dolphins. They appeared to be in a playful mood—swimming, rising and diving, looping and corkscrewing through the clear waters, chasing one another in exuberant shows of friendly competition and jest.

The dolphins were obviously aware of my presence all along, but like the manta rays they seemed unperturbed by that fact. I floated effortlessly, quiet and still, watching them with rapt attention. Several of the dolphins swam quite close, checking me out and reading me with undeniable intelligence and perceptiveness. Like the whale, there was so much that was immediately revealed by the penetrating knowingness of their eyes; eyes emanate the light and spark of Life, the essence and energy of the living awareness that we all share.

I began diving down, then swimming upward, twirling and undulating in a way that I thought would reflect the spirit of their play. I didn't move toward them and was careful to avoid any body language that might be interpreted as threatening. I hoped it would communicate an intention of open friendliness. The invitation appeared to be accepted; the dolphins continued their high-spirited antics all around me, gradually moving closer and closer.

Slowly I began to move in tune with their movements, aligning my body with theirs, turning and propelling myself strongly in the same direction that they swam. They eventually allowed me to swim stomach to stomach, as close as a few feet apart and even seemed to encourage it. I began to feel the dolphins' bodily presence as my own: slick gray and white skin, flexing muscles, perfect bodily form, and awareness—shared awareness, no longer divided, joined.

My mind quieted easily in response to the presence of these inquisitive mammals. All of my attention was given fully to the dolphins; once again it was a return to being entirely in the moment and present. As the dolphins continued to willingly interact with me, and as the play we were sharing became more and more in sync, everything else began to melt away. The amazing feeling of wonder, of opening and cracking the shell of "me" was taking over, and a familiar expansiveness began to unfold, a moving beyond the limitation of thought into a liberating and empowering sense of Oneness and gratitude.

As my usual stream of thoughts continued to subside and as the habitual feeling of being separate from everything around me diminished even more, I shifted into that state of knowing without thought. I knew without a doubt that this ocean of life and my life are one. It is not a comprehension that relates directly to information or facts about life in a biological or textbook sense; it is instead a pure, unfiltered, and immediate knowing of Oneness. It is the wave recognizing that it is not only one with and inseparable from the Ocean, but with all other waves as well.

I continued to experience an occasional and residual sense of separateness from the dolphins, but in a less solid or sure way. The sense of distinction to which I was so accustomed had been relinquished enough for the dividing lines between self and dolphin to soften and intermittently disappear.

It is important to point out that unity experiences like these are more often the exception rather than the rule. It has mostly been that way for me over the years—until recently. More often than not, unity experiences like these will be stifled or blocked entirely by the hardwired habits and conditioning of our thinking minds—or by trying to make the experience happen. Instead of experiencing the simple joy of interacting with another life form without thinking about it, we often succumb to the habit of projecting and superimposing our thoughts, wants, expectations, and fears over the experience—losing any chance for real connection or spontaneity.

When shifting into flow, wonder, or high peak states, we are simply returning to our natural and fundamental state of awareness before our minds have the chance to divide the world into isolated parts. It is then that we can discover the true meaning and beauty of wholeness.

Panama

Moving from Hawaii to Central America—the next two experiences took place while exploring Panama at different times.

Shark's Island

Off the Pacific Coast of Panama there is an infamous island called Isla Coiba. For many years it was a place renown for being a kind of Central American Alcatraz, but much darker. This island prison was a repository for the most heinous criminals in the country and came to be feared for its looming malevolence. Isla Coiba is now a World Heritage Site, but in its day, its prisoners were free to roam. At night the guards would actually lock themselves inside fortified cement buildings, while the prisoners went about unrestrained, doing as they pleased.

From written accounts of the island's prison history, it sounds like life was a very stark survival of the cleverest, an anarchic *Lord of the Flies*-sort of drama. So the possibility of escape was there for prisoners if they were willing to brave the sometimes extremely rough, shark-filled waters surrounding them. But the island is a considerable distance from the mainland, so that route to freedom was exceedingly unlikely without hijacking a boat from unsuspecting sailors passing too close to the island, ignorant of the awaiting danger. According to the stories told at the park's visitors center, most escape attempts took place under the cover of night. But unfortunately for the prisoners, sharks normally feed at night. A prisoner swimming and splashing urgently in an attempt to intercept a passing boat was an easy target, or so the story goes.

Now to be fair to the sharks and clear about their actual behavior: The stories about murderers and rapists being devoured by ravenous sharks are good ones—instant karma—but shark attacks are incredibly rare, statistically speaking. We are not on a shark's normal menu, not nearly as tasty as a nice plump fish or seal. My guess is that many of the prisoners ended up drowning in their escape efforts, and then likely were eaten by an array of other sea critters. Perhaps a shark or two may have taken a few bites, but only in the spirit and excitement of a community meal.

I visited Isla Coiba a few years ago to explore the transparent waters and life-filled reefs around the island. The sharks are still there—numerous and healthy. I'll never forget the first time I put a mask and snorkel on and peered down into the reef below. There were at least three good-sized (two- to three-meters long) black-tipped reef sharks right there, cruising the coral like imperturbable sentinels. I haven't been too many other places where sharks are that easily spotted and so seemingly unconcerned about the presence of humans.

It is such a heart-wrenching and deeply sad story to hear about the continued slaughter of these irreplaceable predators simply for the sake of a bowl of soup made only from their fins. Once the fins are cut, the rest of the animal is left to die a torturous death, thrown back into the ocean to slowly drown. That is a form of separative, self-centered consciousness at its absolute worst. As sharks continue to disappear, the declining health of our oceans will worsen as a consequence of that loss.

Sharks truly possess an aura of ancient and natural perfection. In person and up close they are undeniably sleek, finely tuned and honed predatory wonders. These sharks I was peering at were about three meters below me, gradually slicing graceful circles around the reef. I slowly followed with mask, snorkel, and fins—moving with deliberate ease so as to avoid creating any sense of threat. I'd once had a shark approach me while snorkeling and that memory remained fresh. It was only curious and wanted to know what the splashing was about. Once it saw me and figured out I wasn't a potential meal, it swam away quickly.

This experience was completely different. I filled my lungs with a deep breath before diving down to swim with them and intentionally created a sense of stillness and calm in my mind, body, and demeanor. I know the sharks were sensing and reading me through sensory pathways outside the realm of what humans are normally capable of perceiving. One way sharks sense what is in their environment is through extremely sensitive electrical fields that emanate from their bodies, detecting a much wider range of sensory impressions than many other life forms. They were tuning in and sizing me up, and they decided I wasn't a threat.

I followed the sharks' graceful flowing movements, spellbound in that place where time disappears. As I swam alongside them, fitting my movement and speed as best I could to their inimitable, elegant flow, my mind's running commentary stilled with ease as the moving beauty of the sharks shifted me into awed silence. This, along with my genuine respect and admiration, were the ideal conditions for letting go of self and melding into the presence and energy of this magnificent expression of life. The sharks' acceptance of my nearness to them seemed to grow—even changing to a subtle curiosity. Here, again, looking into the eyes of these creatures heightened the experience. I never tire of gazing at those windows into the depths of our shared life force and awareness. In the meeting of eyes, we can truly know Oneness.

Instead of only experiencing my thoughts, labels, and ideas about these sharks, I was able to turn down the noise of my mind enough to become fully present and tuned into them with my whole being. And with that kind of presence, one's entire experience transforms: Consciousness expands and connects to something bigger. Time and self open up, and the point that I call "myself" becomes all points, everywhere and all at once—now including the sharks. This is Oneness known directly through presence, freed from the normal limitations of the thinking mind. To experience and know another living being in this way is to learn to love Life as both infinite and finite. It is the priceless wisdom of Oneness.

Millions of Minnows

Another vivid experience occurred in a different region of Panama called the San Blas archipelago. San Blas is a chain of islands on the Atlantic side of the country mostly inhabited and governed independently by an indigenous people called the Kuna. I was staying at an eco-resort run by a Kuna family and decided one morning to explore a small reef that was only about twenty or so meters from shore.

As I dove below the clear liquid blue with only mask and fins, I immediately came face-to-face with a massive school of finger-sized, silver gleaming minnows. Thousands of tiny sparks of life moved in perfect harmony and rhythm, shining, and glinting rhythmically with the sun's shifting rays. The school swam as a flawless, orchestrated whole; numberless individual fish seemed to transform into a single life form—indefinable but one. I swam toward them slowly and silently, without the startling noises created by breathing through a snorkel. When I reached the edge of this wall of life, they smoothly and calmly engulfed me; it felt like being swallowed by some enormous, shape-shifting mouth. Each minnow acted in unison to surround and completely envelop me.

Once inside this cocoon of minnows, nothing could be seen but a depthless cloud of silver, with only occasional glimpses of light from the sun at the surface and light reflected off the sea bottom. My awareness, my whole being was wrapped warmly and enraptured by the feeling of being totally surrounded by and one with this shimmering profusion of life. It was easy to come to a silent awareness and wonder-filled joy. I surfaced for air by floating upward, moving my arms and legs as little as possible. Then I would dive back down into their midst, once again encircled by their vital radiance—little jewels of life force—a collective intelligence. It's amazing how long I was able to hold my breath in that state of marvel. It seemed like a long time that was no time.

With my thoughts subsiding, my awareness began to open up to the novel possibilities of perception and feeling that become accessible in that state of stillness. The usual perceived borders of skin, bone, and muscle began to relax, lighten, and become like water. The warm silky surround of the water encouraged a feeling of merging into the school's enormity. My movement became their movement, one and the same. I slowly swam circles and spirals at their center, and they followed. Or was I shadowing them?

I lost all sense of direction and orientation, but I still felt completely comfortable and at home in the heart of this living dance of energy, awareness, life, and light. I was a part that had recognized its Oneness with the larger whole.

Chapter 4 – Experiences of Oneness from My Life

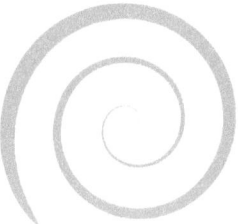

Part Two
Discovering Oneness at the Edge

There is nothing like facing a sudden, life-threatening danger—or at least the real possibility of it—to bring one instantly to the present moment. Some people intentionally seek out and savor the rush of dangerous situations just for that reason: They desire to come as close as possible to the edge of life and death. Most of these thrill seekers, such as free climbers (climbing with no safety gear), face jumpers (plunging off sheer cliff faces with only a parachute), giant wave riders, along with those who partake in any of the "extreme" sports, don't have an actual death wish, but glory in circumstances where death is a very likely outcome if something goes wrong. Total presence is absolutely necessary.

Of course, when walking any edge (and that edge can vary from person to person and from activity to activity), the real need for fully focused attention is usually enough to cause us to still our mind's self-talk and center on what is immediate and now. A temporary state of self-forgetting may happen automatically; laser concentration and a sense of the whole often emerge simultaneously. Along with these shifts in consciousness, there is frequently a healthy dose of adrenaline, plus our brain's endogenous euphoria-producing substances pouring into and electrifying our bloodstreams. But it is that sudden intense presence and feeling of no self, of limitless self, that I believe is the more powerful aspect of the experience. The euphoria-producing brain chemicals are just icing on the cake.

What follows are some of the unity experiences I have had while mountain biking, snowboarding, surfing, and to a lesser extent, rock climbing. Although reaching a certain level of proficiency with any of these sports (or any sport for that matter) is helpful in terms of being open to the possibilities of Oneness, especially the flow state, it is by no means a guarantee. What is undeniably important though is to have gained a sufficient level of skill so that the thought-filled and self-judgmental phase of the learning process has largely passed. Then it is more a matter of setting and sticking with an intention to still the mind and return to natural presence, while the body is fully active and dynamic.

I am not an expert in any of these sports, but that is the beauty of unity experiences: the edge or that point where we feel competent enough to act without thinking about it—to just do it—is potentially open to all of us. Flow can happen at almost any level of ability as long as we recognize and can ride that edge.

However, sometimes danger simply comes—to rock our world and bring us back to the present moment—instantly. This next story is that.

Glacier's Giant Surprise

While camping and hiking in Glacier National Park, Montana, with my girlfriend, we had decided to hike a big loop recommended by a park ranger for being out of the way, less traveled, and good for seeing a wide variety of wildlife. We had been hiking a single-track trail for an hour or so, through dense coniferous forest and a green tangle of alpine shrubs. It was the time of year when many of the mountain berries were beginning to ripen: abundant raspberries, huckleberries, thimbleberries, along with wildflowers of several kinds—scatters of living colors high and low.

Chapter 4–Experiences of Oneness from My Life

As we neared the tree line, we stepped off the trail to take in the amazing snow-tinged mountains and open vistas. I reached down to pull my camera out of its case and was stopped by the biggest pile of fresh, seed-filled dung I'd ever seen. Immediately I recognized that this mound was way too big to have come from a black bear. I knew at once what animal had left this literally steaming pile.

Quickly and instinctively I looked up and right there, less than forty meters away, was a huge, burly, and belligerent-looking grizzly bear walking straight for us. A shock of supercharged energy and ancient fear surged from the center of my body outward, rattling me to my core. Luckily we didn't succumb to the sheer terror and panic that was banging on the door, ready and willing to come out. Amazingly, along with the rising fear, there was also an awestruck admiration and respect. This animal was a healthy, powerful giant, a beautiful living example of its kind; it was real, free to do as it pleased, now less than thirty meters away—striding intently and unstoppably toward us.

My mind went blank, but not in a stupefying or paralyzing way. Instead, as the grizzly drew closer, there was an instantaneous push into intense awareness and readiness. Adrenaline gushed into my veins, and I felt incredibly present and immediate. In as normal a voice as I could muster, I told my girlfriend to walk quickly up the trail, to act as calmly as possible, and definitely not to run or look back. I followed close behind, only glancing sideways to keep an eye on the grizzly but avoiding any threatening or direct eye contact.

This bear obviously had no fear of people, which made the situation potentially more dangerous. And on top of that, he (or she) looked a bit grumpy and not entirely happy with our presence. It also wasn't long prior to this encounter that we had watched the Herzog documentary *Grizzly Man*; it did not have a happy ending.

How does this grizzly encounter fit in with respect to having an experience of Oneness? It's a paradox of sorts. On one hand, there was an obvious and instinctual fear coursing through my entire being—that prehistoric, deeply embedded primordial fear of being clawed, bitten, mauled, and possibly eaten alive by many hundreds of pounds of predator. Even more, there was the fear of my girlfriend being attacked and me being unable to do anything to help. We had no type of deterrents with us, not that it would have made a whole lot of difference if this bear meeting had suddenly turned bad.

Where's the Oneness now? There is only a very clear and real fear of my "self" or my girlfriend coming to a painful and unpleasant end (this is when having an ego, a sense of a separate self that needs and wants to be protected makes 100 percent sense!). But ironically, at the same time that there is a self, a life that wants protecting, wants to live, there is also an intense presence, a forgetting of self, an alertness and keenness brought about by the very real possibility of death or severe injury; it is an extremely simplifying and clarifying fear. Nothing else could possibly have mattered more than that moment. There was not a whole lot of room for extraneous thoughts or worries—only complete attention to what was happening. And it is in those moments when the habit of self is temporarily and necessarily disengaged—despite the fear of that same "self" coming to an abrupt end.

The utter aliveness that comes over you in an encounter of this kind is difficult to express. I imagine it to be similar to what soldiers feel during intense battle. All that is important, all that matters is right action coming from a place before rational thought—before panic. And I was certainly not beyond the potential for panic. I'd never had an experience like this one and had no way of knowing how I would react. Fortunately for all involved, there was an immediate focus and a tuning in to the demands of the moment. Fear in a mostly bodily sense was obviously experienced, but so was presence, instinct, and a spontaneous action flowing clear and unimpeded by unnecessary thought.

Although the grizzly continued to follow us for another mile or so, in and out of sight—most likely because we were in its trail and in the way—it all turned out well. We soon ran into a group of hikers with big cans of hot pepper spray strapped to their waists. They were all more than happy and willing to make a lot of noise once they too saw the grizzly coming toward them (and no, I am not naïve enough to believe the hot pepper spray would have made a bit of difference). As the bear slowly walked by, it glanced over at all of us as we were yelling and shaking our arms madly, not looking the least bit impressed or scared by our efforts. I got the distinct impression of a "you got lucky" look in the grizzly's eyes as he rambled unfazed past us. And, of course, my thinking mind was quickly back and quite ready to comment on and interpret the experience.

Riding on Perfect Circles

For many years mountain biking has been a portal for me into the flow and wonder states, and sometimes for entering into deeper unity experiences as well. But it is also a sport that has been incredibly challenging in terms of being able to genuinely let go of constricting ideas and expectations of how the biking experience "ought" to be. Part of that comes from a stubborn and ingrained competitiveness—with myself as much as with other bikers. To constantly carry the nagging desire to be better, faster, and fearless is the kind of attitude and tension that actually creates a barrier to unity states, and it is these ego-driven motivations that can seriously dampen any chance of spontaneity or depth. Moreover, these kinds of unrealistic expectations layered over the biking experience require an inordinate amount of energy and attention to maintain, distracting from being fully in the moment. Gratefully, I have lightened up considerably over the years.

With all the above being said, it is plain to see that not all rides are conducive to flow or any of the other unity experiences. In other words, I don't just hop on the bike and magically and immediately get into the groove. I have been biking for most of my life and there have been countless rides where I have been overly preoccupied with some irritating desire, concern, or petty worry and unable to still my mind enough to even begin to open to that ever-sweet flow. It can be incredibly aggravating, but the very roots of that frustration are those expectations that I incessantly try to force on the experience, along with all the ways I attempt to control what is happening or what might happen.

On the other hand, when the ride goes right, when the thinking stops, when it all comes together and transforms into an energized and selfless flow, it is a remarkable and unforgettable transformation. Suddenly there is a spontaneous reconnection to the Oneness that is our underlying source and power. It just happens, and this is the difficult part to express if it hasn't been experienced firsthand. It is that moment when one has become so immersed in the action at hand that there is a natural self-forgetting, an unhindered and free-flowing letting go of the need and habit to force, control, or make the biking experience be or feel any way other than what it is.

It all simply falls into place naturally and "clicks"; biker, bike, and all that before was a "part" of the experience becomes one—a unified experience. Wave recognizes its true ground as Infinite Ocean and as one with all other waves, with earth, stone, tree, wind, and sky. This is when the magic begins, but a magic that is simply our innate way of being, our essential and truer nature and our optimal state for being and acting in the world.

Here is how the flow and wonder states often happen and feel for me while mountain biking (taken from various journal writings): First, with biking in general, all the important elements are there for quieting the mind and becoming present. I usually begin a ride by directing my attention to focus on the meditative cadence of my pedaling, on the motion of rolling tires flowing in perfect circles over earth and rock. The trick is to give the mind something to be attentive to other than its constant chatter. I also become concentrated on discovering the line of least resistance, the easiest, smoothest, and most fluid path for biker and bike, whether climbing a steep and rocky single track or descending an eroded, boulder-strewn fire road.

As my body warms and my breath begins to deepen, there is an increasing immersion into the building rhythm of expanding and contracting lungs and heart, into the flexion and extension of muscle and the sharpened acuity of the senses. With this intensifying focus, the habitual mind noise begins to subside and there is a natural movement of awareness out of the isolated and limited "self in the head" into the more expansive space of the entire body and beyond. It is an "embodied presence" and it starts to expand.

Bike becomes an extension of the body, and the body opens to a Oneness with all that surrounds it. The thinking that does occur is simply witnessed, turned to what is immediate and present to the senses then dropped: the topography and feel of the trail, potential hazards, or people nearby—what's going on around me taken as a whole. But this too slowly settles and a higher-level intuition and know-how takes over. It is knowing and feeling without thinking; it is the beginning of flow.

My consciousness switches from its usual separative mode to a more unitive way of seeing and acting in the world; my mind clears, fears drop, and every move, every action happens in and of itself—pure unimpeded spontaneity. Riding becomes smart and efficient, relaxed but powerful. As another kind of intelligence takes over, my totality begins to move in full balance and harmony with the bike and its path. Every maneuver, every turn is felt and savored fully. As the flow state emerges and becomes primary, every rock, root, rut, crack, crevice, bump, and drop-off, every challenge in the terrain is anticipated and responded to with an effortless effort, without thinking about it, without distraction. The experience is full-bodied, carnal, and appreciated in an intensely whole-being way. I feel it everywhere—like I'm tapping into some youthful fire and unlimited energy. Awareness opens and all is felt and experienced as one, as a vital, radiant, and energetic wholeness. It is an energy that fills my heart and lights my being.

Often, after the high-energy action and absorption of the biking flow state, I stop to rest and take it all in. During these breaks, a shift into the wonder state will sometimes happen. The complementary opposite to flow is the wonder state. With the stilling of action and the easing of concentrated attention, consciousness is in a perfect state to expand further—to open and become receptive.

As an energized stillness takes hold, I'm flooded with immense feelings of gratitude, belongingness, and amazement at the absolute miracle of existence. You might say: Well, those feelings are just the leftover adrenaline and the brain's pleasure center turned from action and focus to stillness and openness. And, of course, that is true in part; we are, after all, physical, electrical, and biochemical beings, but that is only a tiny fraction of the story. The larger part is that we are also conscious beings, and that consciousness has the potential to expand into higher states and into new worlds of experience.

Slide!

Snow sports, mostly skiing and snowboarding, have been a part of my life since I was a kid. I started out skiing and then, partly because of my love for surfing, switched to snowboarding. There has been no turning back. My dad and stepmother are both skiers and there is no shortage of friendly jabs back and forth about the lack of credibility and sensibility on the "other side." My father (and stepmother for that matter) won't hesitate to take out a disrespectful or wiseass snowboarder with one of their poles or at least give them a good whack if they can get at them.

I mostly snowboard in the backcountry now, not to get away from my folks' humorous disdain for snowboarders, but because of the high cost of resort skiing and the often chaotically crowded ski slopes. And more important, there is a much better chance of finding some peace and quiet in the backcountry—fewer distractions, more focused attention, ultimately meaning more opportunities for expanding shifts of awareness. For the last several years I have kept a journal of some of these snowboarding experiences, and what follows are short fresh-to-memory entries. Sometimes I float between present tense and past tense because some moments come back more vividly than others—perhaps because they arose from the powerful energizing effect that unity experiences impart on mind and body.

Most all of these snowboarding adventures took place in the pristine backcountry of Vail Pass above Vail, Colorado; Buffalo Pass outside of Steamboat Springs, Colorado; and at Hidden Valley in Rocky Mountain National Park—all of which have an excellent mix of conditions and terrain. From open, treeless alpine mountaintops, to pine tree- and aspen-filled glades, to smooth, steep bowls or boulder-strewn chutes, it's all there. Spending time in the wild places of Colorado has created a kind of kinship with these landscapes; it is a relationship that changes and grows year by year.

The described experiences were sometimes solitary, other times they were shared with family and friends. Many of my most memorable recollections have been with my brother. Snowboarding together has been, and continues to be, our way of connecting and sharing a love and camaraderie only brothers can know. Those experiences have been some of the best and closest times we have spent together and for which I will always be tremendously grateful.

Snowboarding lends itself perfectly to opening and entering into the flow and wonder states, as well as encouraging dips into deeper unity states or Oneness. Similar to mountain biking and surfing, snowboarding involves and demands a skilled, coordinated dynamic between the human element and the greater powers of energy, gravity, earth, wind, water, and sun. But unique to snowboarding is snow, that fantastically strange and peculiar state of water that adds an incredibly novel dimension to life in the colder climes. One of snow's wondrous attributes, with the help of gravity obviously, is its natural capacity for reducing friction, along with its matchless ability for helping to produce a sliding and gliding motion. In that potential for accelerated and fluid movement are the hidden possibilities for unity experiences.

People often talk about the wonders of skiing or boarding untracked powder; I questioned this at one point in my life, but never again. Powder is snow in its most sublime and beloved form, at least for anyone who has truly partaken in its magic. When it is pristine, unblemished, perfectly and sensuously smooth, and deliciously sculpted, powder provides unequaled opportunities for entering into an active flowing stillness and expansiveness. Add to that the rush of buttery carved turns through a tree-adorned snowscape and there's nothing like it. When it is trackless powder, it is purity incarnate—untouched and virgin, so inviting, sensual, and soft; something about powder's purity just draws, calls, and beckons for it to be touched, carved, and painted in sinuous curves of elation.

Here are a few of those experiences taken from various journal entries.

I stand atop a mountain ridge in the center of a circling embrace of the majestic Rocky Mountains. Snow-frosted peaks of every imaginable shape and size form a sweeping expanse, vast and magnificent. Breathing deep and peering into this unparalleled beauty immediately opens heart and spirit to a greater whole and wonder. It is that immense mountain presence that sets the stage for moving into flow and Oneness. It is genuine perfection as it is, untouched and unaltered by the thinking mind.

The day is crisp, radiantly clear, and shining. No one is around, just my brother and me. The moment of taking off, of beginning a descent into the unknown brings me to the Now. It is an opening moment, charged with anticipation and excitement. Warming to the flow is slow at first. But as I concentrate on discovering the best pathway down through snow-blanketed earth, boulders, pines, and giant aspens, presence begins to return. The snow is waist deep, light, and fast. The descent is steep in parts, easing up, then steep again—perfect for moving more fully into the moment.

As my speed and momentum build, thinking stops, thoughts rise and fall like quickly passing, evaporating clouds—but without "me" attaching to them. My attention shifts to the nuance and detail of the surroundings and to possibility, to the demands of flying down unspoiled mountainsides. My senses fill with the light and form of snow, rock, and tree, with the sound of wind and snow sliding, swishing, and crunching under the board, the smell of pine essence mixed with cold, slightly moist air wafting over and into me. All of this unfolds with only a few wisps of thought.

The sun's white fire lights the snow as I slice through its powdery thickness, illuminating and electrifying it, creating a boundless sea of luminescent, shimmering diamonds, each burning and shining with vast star power. Weightless, floating turns carry my awareness through this sea of radiance, the powder bursting upward as the edges of my board catch and turn. I hear and feel this mist of frozen crystalline spray flying into the breeze as it is liberated from its snow-packed hold. As the snow moves into the air and sky around me, it releases the wet scent of trees and of a wintery earth. It is an essence and moistness that enters my nose and floods my being; it's an ancient smell that is carried deep into my mind and memory, becomes me.

No thoughts; they have disappeared like the raised clouds of snow behind me. My normally bounded sense of self is unchained, set free; the "me" that is human awareness is freed and opened, spilling out into the infinity of pure Awareness that is its Source. I unwind and discover a larger Oneness in this beautiful flowing, sinuous dance downward.

No time for thinking about the next turn, the next move or maneuver. Only this precious moment that is timeless.

As I float over and down this snow-covered mountainside—into the unknown—a lightness begins to emerge, a lightness of form, mind, heart, and a lightness of being—pure energy. Time recedes, space melts, awareness moves out from behind my eyes and into every felt cell of my body and beyond. It is a move out of the mind into the more expansive space of bigger awareness. Discovered in those moments of liberating speed and motion is an ecstatic jubilation and gratitude, yet realized in and through a center of stillness. It is a snow-flowing celebration and the profoundest appreciation of existence itself.

☙

On Vail Pass there is a narrow bowl that we have come to know well and to respect. It is super steep at its entry points, with high, tree-lined sides lining the entire way down. The take-off zones are precipitous and fast but the descent gradually eases up toward the bottom. On top of this bowl there often sit huge and heavy cornices ready to wreak havoc at the slightest provocation, like monstrous kings perched on their thrones, waiting to wage war. We sometimes just call this particular bowl the chute. The path of the chute is kept clear of trees by elemental forces and . . . avalanches. That possibility definitely adds a factor of intense alertness to riding this run.

We are always careful, aware, and only enter from openings on both sides of the bowl, avoiding the drop-off and cornices at the top—knowing that they are avalanche triggers. We also carry location beacons and other safety gear. The chute is north facing, so colder and in the shade, making the snow lighter and faster. Because of the avalanche danger, we usually board down at the edge of the tree-bordered sides, out of the slide zone for the most part. It feels to me like surfing a giant standing wall of snow.

Chapter 4–Experiences of Oneness from My Life

I ease into the chute carefully from the right side, looking up to the left and getting a feel for the potential avalanche danger looming above, but keeping my speed up. During this sideways approach, the wall of snow that I am traversing is steep enough to run my hand along, like caressing a wave in the ocean while surfing. The moment is powerful, one-pointed, but spacious. At first it feels like a precursory waiting and preparation, a gauging and building up, a revving up. Then it's just full-on release, letting go, a freeing, open-ended freefall, soaring into the unknown. The snow is perfect, only a few tracks—fast, light, alive—a shimmering, snowy luminosity. This is it! No separateness. I'm unplugged, disengaged, the "me" left behind.

I cruise through the spaces between trees, reveling in the challenge of finding the right path instantly and floating flawlessly over billowing pillows of snow, tracing the natural impressions created by tree wells and boulders. The trees! A living presence and an intimate part of the dance. As the state of flow deepens, awareness opens and it becomes easier to recognize the precious vital force and elemental awareness that suffuses all life—animate and inanimate. That is the energy that I am.

At the bottom of the chute I stop; I take a moment to relax and receive, to surrender to and fully enjoy an uncontainable exhilaration of the moment. Consciousness changes from the more active state of flow to the stilled contemplative embrace of the wonder state. In that place of wonder there is a taking in of the whole universe in a single moment of silent, clear understanding and a rising feeling of Oneness.

[same place, a different day]

I approach and enter from the left side of the chute, just to the outside of a big section of overhanging cornices. It is steep but the powder holds. Speed comes quickly; turns seem to happen without volition, unwinding in a rise and fall of momentum-created lightness. Time ceases; I am a living, self-aware conduit for the universe, for its energy, for play, and for joy. My awareness becomes both local and nonlocal—everywhere at once. A trace of separateness remains, but it has lost most of its definition and solidness.

As I continue soaring and carving flowing turns downward, the usual distinctiveness of self begins to lighten and loosen. That is the opening. It is the unrivaled feeling that my entirety is simply an extension of all that is around me, as if my individual form has become indistinct from all that surrounds it. Snow, body, board, heart, mind—it all blends, coalesces, becomes one. I am all of this; this is who I am. I have emptied of separateness, become like the flow of water: natural, without effort, immediate, pure, and One. Mind quiet, heart open, judgment suspended, perception expands, and time and space lose meaning. Small-minded awareness transforms into big and open-minded awareness. All that is left is an intense living presence, wild happiness, and ecstatic thankfulness.

Waves of Ecstasy
The Meeting

"Surfing"—I say that word with a deep and utter fondness. Discovering surfing was one of those serendipitous crossroads that changed the course of my life. To this day, it still seems crazy to me how significantly life can be redirected and transformed by one simple decision or by a single act of kindness.

I recall the day it all started with the vividness and clarity of minutes ago. I was walking down a dirt road exploring along the water's edge on a small Caribbean island off the coast of Panama, where I would be living for the next couple of years. Up ahead in the distance, I could see someone loading surfboards onto the top of an old beat-up, rusted greenish-blue Plymouth Duster. As I approached, a young teenage Panamanian walked around from the other side of the car, grinned a big friendly smile, and in clear Spanish-accented English, asked if I wanted to go surfing. Just like that.

His name is Julito. He had no idea who I was or anything about me, but that simple, open-hearted gesture and invitation began an incredible adventure and a long-lasting, often comical, and always interesting friendship. Julito and I don't see each other that often anymore. It's mostly an occasional online message, but there is always gratitude in my mind when I think back to those times and to his offer of friendship—and my doorway to surfing.

For anyone who has ever given surfing an honest first-time try, it is probably unnecessary for me to say that I got myself unmercifully worked and beaten up that day. And when I say worked, that's an understatement—more like tumbled, twisted, held under water, rolled sideways, head over heels, and every other imaginable way. My nasal passages were jet washed and spotless, cleaner than I thought possible. The waves were only about chest-to-head high, but given my complete lack of experience, they were monsters.

This particular reef break, which is called Black Rock because of the dark, foreboding coral heads that stand nearby and above the ocean like sinister, warning sentries, was an amazing place to learn how to surf. Its saving grace for beginners is that it has a channel to one side that usually offers a safe haven if you haven't already been sucked too far into the break. Black Rock has both left and right running waves, but on big days the lefts can and will take you into sea urchin-encrusted shallow and sharp reef if you don't get out of the wave in time. The right, on the other hand, unfurls toward a mostly calm channel. Of course, I often went left because I was convinced it was easier being the left-footed surfer that I am (when the left foot is placed at the back of the board—commonly referred to as goofy foot). Needless to say, there were times when I paid with flesh, blood, and fear.

I began surfing in my late twenties, which is considered a late start by many. To learn how to surf well and to surf in waves that are sometime double overhead is by far one of the most difficult challenges I have ever attempted. And by that I mean just getting to an intermediate level. I use the verb "is" instead of "was" given that many times when I get back into the water and it has been a while, it feels like I'm starting from scratch. Each time out is new, different, and for me there is almost always an edgy feeling, which is good; it keeps me aware and attentive. Surfing may look easy, but that illusion is quickly dispelled when the waves start getting bigger, burlier, and meaner. To actually master surfing is a whole other story. There are many super-talented surfers out there who make it look simple, but I'm sure most have some horror stories about getting to that point.

Surfing can be a genuine test of one's mettle and fortitude. It pushes and challenges a person—body, mind, heart, and spirit. I learned early that physical conditioning is absolutely critical in order to gain any real level of proficiency, confidence, or comfort in the water, especially in bigger surf. A little bit of craziness and the ability to relax when your mind is ready to panic is also helpful. I quickly figured out the importance of being able to hold my breath when being held underwater for what seems like an eternity (which is probably only about twenty seconds when your heart is pounding and every cell in your body is screaming for oxygen).

Also vital is learning how to act from the gut instantly, to feel what is right and wrong instinctively, to sense dangers, obvious and hidden; to know one's limits and fears without having to continually run those associated thoughts through the mind. These abilities are the foundation of the flow state. Hesitation in bigger surf is a real danger. An immediate knowing, with no vacillation about when to go and when not to go, is critical. I have had way too many hard lessons beat into me from "thinking" that I should just go for it. As the famous bumper sticker says, "Eddie would go." Eddie Aikau was a Hawaiian hero, famed as a fearless and skilled pioneer of big wave surfing and water rescue. To reach that level of heroic skill and intuition requires long hours in the ocean, to the point of gaining an instantaneous know-how and flow.

The "spirit" aspect of surfing is about the experience of Oneness that is possible in the ocean when fully present and in a state of heightened consciousness. Being rooted and centered in presence is the key that enables a surfer to more easily join with the energy of the water, the waves, and the raw power of the elemental forces that move them. By being fully attentive to and aligned with those wonders and powers of the ocean, there arises the possibility of "tapping the Source," of finally glimpsing and feeling the bigger picture, the deeper unifying reality that is the creative wellspring of all that we are and all that exists. To me, it is this experience of surfing that is the essence of the expression "soul surfing." The ocean is the perfect place to realize directly the Oneness of Life in both a worldly and transcendent sense—and why I am so partial to the Ocean and Wave metaphor.

Spiritual realization in this way is the inherent possibility we all possess to wake up to a higher and unifying level of consciousness. Surfing is a doorway to experience in microcosmic form the immensities and mysteries of the universe that often seem overwhelming in their enormity. It is a pathway to reconnect in a life-size scale to that which may mostly seem intangible and beyond reach or comprehension because of its absolute vastness. And when you finally catch that first wave and lose your "self" in that gliding ride along the face of a glassy translucence, the door opens, the cosmic rabbit hole appears, and for most people there is no turning back. The incomparable joy is felt for only moments but emblazoned in the heart for a lifetime.

Look at the uncontainable passion that shines in the eyes of surfers when they are talking about their sport. It is that irrepressible "stoke" and fire that burns inside like a fever, but a fever that feels so good, so damn fantastic that all you want afterwards is more. There is the danger of it becoming an obsession—turning into a delirium if the fire is not tamed and balanced. Those tastes of Oneness are some of the most intensely satisfying experiences on the planet, and sometimes it's just plain impossible to control a fire like that.

Surfing has been a key catalyst for me in terms of understanding what it means to have an experience of Oneness. I was hugely fortunate to learn where and when I did. What follows are entries from a journal of surfing experiences written within the last five years, although I have been keeping a log of these kinds of experiences for much longer—over twenty years.

The Beauty of Place, the Beginning of Oneness while Surfing

The ocean reflects the elemental energies of water, sky, earth, and sun in all their primordial power, mixed and rising with Life's pulsing energies. Amid those ancient creative forces I float here in these clear, warm, shimmering turquoise waters imbibing a giant panorama; there is a felt infinity in the horizon, where ocean joins sky. In the far distance are mysterious, darkly looming clouds and mist-shrouded volcanic mountains blanketed by the lushest living greens. Closer by, lining the coast, there stands a wildness, a verdant wall of tropical jungle that shines in an even deeper emerald hue. Ancient sounds of life and the ocean's primal briny moistness and richness reach me, carried by the rising mist of nearby pounding surf. The songs of birds and insects, the hum and thrum of their daily lives speak to me familiar and comforting rhythms.

Seabirds traverse the waves of wind rising and falling above the surf. Below in the crystalline waters is a rich tapestry of rainbow-colored life—corals, sea fans, sponges, Caribbean fish, and a diverse profusion of other sea life—dancing sparks of color everywhere.

Pelicans (I call them *los hermanitos*—little brothers) often glide along the wind currents generated in front of a cresting wave; beautiful and inspiring flight up close. Instinctively I connect with these prehistoric-looking creatures. They seem to be the ocean made flesh, in the form of feathers, muscle, blood, bone, and awareness. I imagine my essence merging with their essence; I feel in a very real way the rush of their gliding flight, the pulse of beating heart, living vitality, and the way all senses are so intimately tuned to the ocean. We are one; we share the same pure, spacious awareness and the same life flow; it is the Oneness of Life's greater awareness expressing itself in endlessly novel ways.

Oneness in Waves—Discovered and Rediscovered

After a short boat ride, I am dropped off on a small island just across from the main island that is a part of the archipelago of Bocas del Toro where I first lived more than twenty years ago. I step off the dock onto a sandy path that weaves through a scattering of tropical homes on stilts, around the island and toward the open ocean. I walk slowly, consciously tuning into the rich array of island sights, sounds, and smells that begin to open my mind: ocean scents rich with salty life, wet sand, decomposing piles of fallen tropical leaves, mud and decay mixed with the fresh ocean breezes. Caribbean dishes fried and baked drift invitingly through the warm, humid air like the coconut palms themselves are emanating the food's delicious smells.

It is time to turn down the thoughts and to realign with the energies of the island, the rhythms of its life and the ocean. The usual excited anticipation that helps me get out of my head and into the wider awareness of my whole body begins to take hold. I have been coming back to these islands for so many years now. Each time is new and feels like finally returning home to a best friend or a lover who has been on my mind and in my heart. It is a beauty that blew me away long ago, entered and changed me. Each return is a reunion, a love deepened.

As I draw nearer to the break, I begin to hear and feel the rumble of the waves crashing, and start to taste and drink in that lusty sea mist that wets the beach and palms with a thick salty dew. I climb up a grass- and tree-covered coral outcropping that overlooks the break. The wide vista never fails to catch me and surprise me with wonder. I stand at the top meditatively, gratefully, with the silent intention to center, prepare, and open to the deeper possibility of connection and Oneness I know I might uncover here.

The waves roll in along both sides of the overlook, unwinding with a satisfyingly smooth and sinuous form, shining in gorgeous shades of greenish blue. There is such a moving beauty and resonant aliveness to them. I feel it in my whole being—touching, pulling, and calling me. As the waves unwind I sense their embodied rhythm, feel the vibration as they crash. I draw in the ancient, blood-stirring smell of sea spray and ocean; its feminine essence fills me.

I return to that place of vast gratitude. Thank you—from my depths. I feel in my core a reverence and awe and the recognition that life and death are inseparable. I know that this body is mortal but my being is infinite—not a disembodied soul or spirit, but the pure awareness that is both the unique wave and the infinite ocean. It is a feeling that is so near, as close as my breath, but so often just out of reach. Thoughts come and go, interspersed with stillness, and then a purposeful return to breath and presence.

I enter the churning ocean with the utmost respect, with a center that is primed and calm, brought out by an intentional stillness and attentiveness to the moment. The water, warm and thick feeling, softly envelops my body. I understand fully the idea of ocean as feminine, as nurturing, as fertile and sensuous—as Mother Ocean. Her waters have an old familiarity that stirs the life-giving waters in my own veins. In these moments, there is only this thin layer of skin separating my liquid essence and energy from its primordial home.

The sensation of water passing over and around my body is invigorating. The saltwater, so close in composition to the liquid life essence that courses through my body, nurturing its millions of cells, eases the seemingly solid border between skin and sea—as if they were communicating their still present affinity for each other. My usual sense of having a defined, concrete physical boundary diminishes and my body begins to feel as if it is merging with the ocean. There is an opening to Oneness in that feeling.

Before I paddle out, there is again a reverential acknowledgment and another offering of thanks, a bowing before the sheer power of the ocean and the tremendous force and energy held in each wave—and the fact that I am in the middle of nowhere and mostly alone. I have experienced nothing else like the rushing and crushing power held in a breaking wave. With that recognition is a deep-seated deference and a rising sense of uncertainty in the unknown that is before me and calling.

Once I am finally able to push through and outside of the crashing chaos of the break's impact zone, I discover an unexpected and peaceful glassiness to the ocean. That striking contrast is almost always the case—and unexpected. I sit up on the board and start to pay attention to all the many details coming in. I watch and I wait and I listen with all senses, homing in on subtle details, getting a feel for what current and wave are doing, how they are interacting, and where the best take-off spot will be in this ever-changing dynamic. Steadily I become readier and more alert. Thoughts arise but I am able to disengage and disentangle from them, watch them, let them come and let them go. The mind stills further and there is a vibrant freshness and aliveness that takes hold.

As I watch the incoming sets, I get a sense of timing and how the waves are breaking. I know where to be, when and how to be. Then I see that certain wave, feel it rolling in, know it's right, and all thoughts cease. An intense flood of energy surges inside my entire body and I begin to paddle like mad, hard and with every fiber of arm, chest, and back. Glancing back at the wave as I paddle, I see it slowly build, moving toward its peak and full rising potential. I feel it take hold of body and board and it is so utterly satisfying. Every particle of my being feels the rising energy—in the vibrating atoms of my body and in those same reverberating atoms of the wave, and that feeling is indescribable. I paddle like it's my last and only wave, not knowing for sure what's next.

If all goes well, if timing, positioning, enough power, and finesse to get into the wave are there, along with a quick, fluid jump to the feet, enough balance to make the drop and if the wave's shape and form are just right—if all of these factors come together and jibe and if I'm able to make the bottom turn back up into the face and the releasing energy of the wave, that is where a deeper flow becomes possible. All of it unfolds as a fluid whole, emptied of thought, but the intensity in the beginning is what potentially brings the flow and wonder states to their fuller realization and expression.

In the face of the wave, there is that pinpointed yet expanded awareness that includes and becomes the unfurling wave. The absorption can be so complete that the sense of a "me" as an individual spatially and temporally distinct from ocean and wave disappears quickly. That is Oneness and flow, and once a person wakes up to that flowing, unified state of consciousness, to that possibility of awareness, life is never the same. It is absolute bliss, sublime beyond words.

Many times, having been totally absorbed in the flow of the surfing experience, I remember coming out of certain waves so jazzed up that I was unable to get back to the details of the ride for a while. In that place where time and self are momentarily transcended—water, wave, energy, form, sense experience, motion, and feeling are all realized as one flowing whole, one consciousness. Duality is seen through to the deeper unity beneath. All senses merge into one sense. Memory in the form of language, as we understand it, has a loose foothold in unified states of consciousness and thus the difficulty encountered in conveying through words (fragments of reality) what is actually experienced as an unbroken continuity.

The Finger, the Moon, and Liquid Bliss

These last few entries are from several years and in no particular order. I share them like the Zen parable of a finger pointing at the moon: ultimately the truth of experiences of Oneness is not to be given but only pointed to; it can only be experienced in one's own deepest being—without words. The door is there for all of us—waiting . . .

As I float half immersed in the Caribbean ocean warmth, the miracle of water fills me and I revel in its lusciously silky, encircling hold. The lighting changes, the clouds clear, and the sky pours its purest blues into the liquid form of ocean. It floats on the flowing emerald waters like a slick of sky. The ocean's surface reflects and moves those colors through ripples of energy and motion. It is hypnotically enchanting in its otherworldly and exotic beauty. The sun burns brighter still and the already rich colors intensify even more, dancing distinct but as one, in rhythm with the unique pulsing aliveness and creative expressiveness that is everywhere, in everything. I am all of this, not separate—One.

I love to peer into the ocean's mirror on the world that is not exact, but abstract. And gliding on a wave's wall of liquid crystal begins to feel like rushing along the outside of a moving, fluid window—a window into the underlying splendor, color, and form of another dimension, one so close but still not touchable.

Most surfers who have been surfing long enough will have forever soaked into memory certain monumental and epically unforgettable waves. These are the waves that are caught when everything is in the right place at the right time, when all elements fall together into a perfect harmony.

This day was one of those days and one of those waves. I sensed its rolling, growing power even at a distance. As the wave drew closer its actual magnitude wasn't immediately apparent. But as it began to rise and crest it suddenly became quiet, and then I knew it was a giant. Often there is a strange, vacuous silence and pausing of time right before a wave builds and climbs to its climax. Then suddenly it's there: Pure graceful power rising like a watery freight train out of nowhere, ready to fire off its long-held and mounting energy.

I felt this wave in the pit of my stomach as it seemed to build slowly, but in a flash it jacked up all at once. I didn't have to paddle hard to get into this wave; it took hold of me like it was hungry for company. In these moments, thinking drops off immediately, the world stops, and the lines of self fall away. Now is all there is and it's astounding

The drop was a floating free fall. I stuck it and powered quickly into the face of a glassy wave that was huge, thick, and way overhead. I felt the crashing, vibrating thunder behind me in every fiber and bone of my body as the wave exploded in a magnificent, ecstatic release. My rhythm was right on and I tuned in instantly to this wave's unique dynamics. The flow had begun.

The wave unfolded so quickly that I had to read its points of highest potential energy without a trace of hesitation; it was an action arising out of intuition, without an internal voice or fear, a deep and easy flow, a rising, falling, flying dance along the wave's face. Ideally a surfer wants to seamlessly and gracefully discover again and again those energetic sweet spots that surge one farther and faster along the wave to its end.

As I coursed in rhythm with the wave's release, my body was freed from the boundaries of self-identity. Ocean, wave, body, mind, heart, and spirit joined as One. It felt as if I was flashing in and out of existence, appearing and disappearing as my awareness merged and flowed with the energy of the breaking wave. The wave's power became my power; my energy became the wave's energy. In that intense presence, there was a taste of Oneness, and it was in that Oneness that love, gratitude, and pure bliss poured forth. At the end of the wave, as I flew over clear waters with coral that seemed inches below me, I let out a hearty, soulful laugh of elation—waves of ecstasy.

Climb to Flow, Flow to Climb

For around five years I lived in the Bluegrass State of Kentucky, during which time I was enthusiastically encouraged to learn how to rock climb. I'm glad I decided to give it a go because I eventually came to see rock climbing's tremendous potential for bringing about unity experiences. What made a big difference as well is that I learned to climb in one of the most amazing places in the country—the Red River Gorge. The impressive high limestone cliffs of the gorge are nestled and hidden within a luxuriant green Appalachian landscape; it is a rich wildness that is stunning and affecting in its ancient, rocky presence. And the climbing is truly phenomenal.

With me still are a few memorable climbs when I was able to enter more fully into the flow and wonder states. But what I also remember well, especially in the beginning, was how often I found myself shaking from head to toe from fear and exhaustion—about as far from flow or Oneness as I could be. The unitive elements of climbing that follow are similar in many respects to those in the other sports described here: I quickly learned that climbing demands a razor-sharp attention to the details of the moment, while simultaneously requiring an awareness that is wide open, centered, relaxed, and able to grasp all that is happening as a larger, unbroken whole, when the left and right hemispheres of the brain begin to work in unison.

The best climbing happens when thinking subsides and the climber moves directly into presence. Regardless of what type of climbing one is involved in, attention to what is immediate and being able to eventually act without thinking too much about it can be critical. Once again, effortless action, free flowing and arising out of a point of inner stillness, is the doorway into unity experiences. Thoughts that create fear, panic, or hasty actions can cause mistakes that deteriorate into dangerous situations quickly. Obviously, like any skill when it is first learned, thought is an essential part of the learning process. With climbing especially, a certain level of skill, particular to each person, must be reached before flow or other unity experiences become possible. It takes time on the rock, energy and patience, and a passion to figure out the climbing dynamic.

To climb well, with assuredness and confidence, a climber's body must be transformed into a temple of core strength; muscles, bones, spine, ligaments, and tendons must all be made strong, powerful, and conditioned with endurance, yet also flexible, supple, and light. The body comes to know and intuit without intervening thoughts the intricacies of flowing, efficient, creative, and coordinated movements—timing.

The mind is trained to disengage and to focus on only what is completely necessary, what is right there and right in that moment. At that point, a climber can often enter that unifying state of consciousness, when the climber, what is being climbed, and the act of climbing become one; when body, mind, heart, and spirit feel like an extension of the rock in front, the earth below, and the sky above. This is when the possibilities of Oneness open up.

I recall one climb in particular when everything fell into place. I had climbed this route a few times previously, so I was familiar with the general sequence of the climb, although not to the point of remembering details about specific moves other than what was clearly in front of me. It was a route that was challenging at the time—what is called a 5.10c in the world of rock climbing and probably considered an intermediate climb by most. At that time I thought of myself as an intermediate climber, having learned to lead climb-bolted routes fairly recently—long enough to have gained the confidence I needed to lead this familiar climb. Falls, even when roped, can shake the hell out of your day depending on how far below the rope is clipped. The fall is usually twice that distance. I had already had a few doozies, and they definitely left their mark.

Most of the climbing I did in the Red River Gorge was sport climbing, which means protective bolts are already in place through the entire climb. The key is being able to clip the rope into those security-giving bolts with ease, fluidness, and in the most efficient way possible. Energy is limited and climbing with energy-saving form and fine-tuned technique is everything. This route was right on the edge of my ability, but not so intimidating as to fill my head with flow-killing and energy-draining thoughts of doubt or hesitation. I felt in the groove with this climb right off—dialed in, present, and ready, which is the perfect mind-body space for more easily entering into unity states, especially flow. I truly love these moments.

Here is a picture of that climb.

I breathe deeply and become grounded, extending my arms and putting my hands slowly and deliberately on the rock, feeling, smelling, absorbing the rocky essence—taking it all in with a quiet intensity and readiness. I sense everything as a connected, interwoven whole: the sounds of insects humming and buzzing, bird song filtering in from all directions, distant voices of other climbers, drifting smells of humid rock and earth, a barely perceptible breeze invisibly rustling a green sea of deciduous hardwoods. A rising scent of humid vegetation and decaying, earthy smells infuse the air—thick enough to taste, viscous enough to feel. I describe it now as separate perceptions and feelings, but when it was happening it was all at once, without words, pure and present.

The feel of the rough, time-worn limestone under my hands fits perfectly, connecting and solid, like my body is entering into the greater, slower awareness of earth and rock. It is cool with spots that are sun warmed and soothing. I shift and balance my weight between my extended arms and legs, which are flexed yet relaxed, finding that perfect, energy-conserving laid-back position and angle. It is a befriending of gravity, finding a lightened accord and fluidity with that mysterious force of nature. Legs and arms move smoothly, easily, and knowingly, finding the optimal holds and balance, one after the other with ease.

My breath rises and falls in rhythm with the upward dance. Hanging the clip and clipping the rope is liquid and graceful, one after another, but seemingly in unison. All of it melds together as a flowing, flawless whole. A few intermittent thoughts arise, mostly just a noticing of detail—more feeling than thinking, but a feeling that is more embracing and far-reaching somehow. I never know for sure when or if the flow state will take hold, but this day it was right on and powerful. My body feels precise, relaxed, and efficient; inner and outer energy flows in perfect harmony and as one with the unfolding moment.

As I climb higher, everything feels magnified; senses are tuned, clear and aware of features minute and grand. The tiniest details of every nook and cranny of rock, ledge, crack, and crevice are taken in and absorbed in slow motion. But again, there is also that big picture intuition in the background. It feels like up, down, and all other directions are one and the same, an unbroken extension of where I am right now; I am a center point that is all points ascending this ancient wall of limestone.

On occasion I pause on a slight ledge to really take it all in, to breathe in and silently imbibe the astonishing nature of this lived moment. I marvel silently in the possibility of this mind and body expressing itself through balanced and muscle-powered movement upward against the ubiquitous pull of gravity downward. In that total presence and reveling is the wonder state.

All senses are heightened and feel to be one; my body is charged; attention is freed from thought and able to enter into the finer energies of all that surrounds me. Emotionally there is a profoundly moving feeling of the beauty and power of this unique place, a primal knowing and joining with the elemental essence of rock, stone, and earth. My totality becomes a channel for this wonder of Big Life and for the wildness that abounds inside and out. In a spiritual sense there is a shifting of consciousness from separation to Oneness, an unspoken understanding of the greater unity below the surface of the multiplicity that our senses tell us insistently is the one and only reality.

While I climb there is an astounding, almost surprised feeling of being in a moment like no other. It is the wonder of being able to "witness" from a higher, wider perspective what we often miss or take for granted in our often limited, self-absorbed view. That is the power of presence, and as always, with that there is an inexpressible gratitude that emanates from the center, pure feelings without words or boundaries of self. In that instant on the rock is an opened heart, a higher wonder, and perfection. It is the Oneness that speaks to us always, from everywhere and nowhere—silent whispers enticing us to enter into its greater possibilities.

Part Three
Drawn to Life and to the Power of Wild Places

A consistent and, I believe, common way for opening into experiences of Oneness is through encounters with animals—domesticated as well as wild. As described in my experiences with life in the ocean, communion with other living beings can offer a readily available opportunity for shifting from our day-to-day busy-mindedness into the lightness and spaciousness of a unifying state of consciousness. Close interactions with animals or other living beings can help us to loosen our conceptual boundaries and the unquestioned beliefs we may hold that impede our connecting with what we normally perceive as the "outside" world. This can be a major step in realizing a larger picture of Oneness.

What is it about experiences with animals then that can help us shift away from our habitual mode of separateness and into a more unified state of mind?

First and foremost, it is the pure, spontaneous, and unencumbered presence that is so truthfully epitomized by and that often shines forth naturally from animals. Animals are always in the Now. It is their nature, as it is also ours underneath our thinking and divisive minds. They are not trying to be, do, or achieve anything other than what they are naturally—no planning, no regrets, and no judgments. And they exemplify living in the Now in a way that makes it continually possible for us to emulate them and learn presence. Fostering a deeper relationship with other life forms allows us to open awareness, unify, connect, and love in a way that is often turned off, dormant, or drowned out by our distracted modern lives.

Perhaps in an even more fundamental way, the relationships we have with animals, whether lasting only minutes or many years, remind us of the wondrous fact of existence itself and the utter miracle of our own human existence. The sheer diversity of life on our big blue planet is mind boggling; it moves us to stop and delight in the incredible creativity of our universe. This knowledge allows us to tune in more easily to the web of Oneness into which all and everything are interwoven. Sadly, the continuing loss of biodiversity on our planet is undeniably one of the greatest and most disturbing, potentially irreversible tragedies of our time.

Sometimes, too, animal encounters simply provide a way to experience the incontrovertible native intelligence and living presence of another creature. It can stop us in our tracks, blast away what we have always thought to be true, and open our minds to new and deeper emotions and understanding. To know experientially, viscerally, and without a doubt that the blood and life energies that course through the bodies of all life is the same living vitality that flows through our veins is true wisdom—the wisdom of Oneness.

One with the Pack

Phoebe became a part of our family when I was ten and left us when I was about twenty-three. She was a white and black spotted English Setter, a breed that I haven't encountered often since her death. We shared thirteen years of companionship, friendship, life wisdom, and a love for each other that is with me still. And I use the word love without fear of projecting human feelings onto her that she was incapable of having. From her side of things, it may not have been love in the way we most often think of the word, but there are many ways that love can manifest in the world—especially in relation to a sense of deep connection and devotion to another living being. She showed that kind of love and deference every day of her life. Dogs, like wolves, are social animals, and I was her pack

Like any relationship, ours changed over time—it moved into deeper territory as I grew in understanding. As I mentioned before, we lived in a fairly rural area of Colorado with easy access to the many wild places around our house. So during our younger years we spent a lot of time enjoying the pure physical rush and thrill of the run, of exploring hills, river valleys, canyons, forests, streams, and caves. It was an unstoppable, overflowing exuberance driven by simple curiosity and the unrelenting desire to know what was around the next bend.

What I see more clearly now is that all the while I was running and stalking in the wilds with Phoebe, I was inadvertently absorbing from her a certain fundamental natural wisdom. As most hunting dogs like her do instinctively, Phoebe would stop frequently to tune into the sensory details of her surroundings. I watched this closely and intuitively started doing the same. I would imagine myself in her body, concentrating intently on all I envisioned her to be sensing. It sometimes felt like some part of me was able to enter into her experience; I realize it was simply a matter of me moving my attention into the greater field of awareness that is shared by all life.

With time, I began to notice that not only did all my senses become keener and more finely tuned, but I also began to develop a capacity for new types of perceptions and feelings. I was learning to find silence, to quiet the internal swirl of thoughts that would normally filter, shape, and often dim my experience of the world. I discovered how to pay attention in both a focused and mind-opening way, to experience without thought or preconceptions every sight, sound, smell, taste in the air, and every feeling perceptible and slight. By stopping often and by listening with my whole body and with my entire being, I was unintentionally gaining the benefits of meditation and cultivating presence without realizing it.

Those early years with Phoebe were instrumental in terms of preparing the ground for later unity experiences. It was the beginning of knowing the feel of flow discovered in those wild abandoned runs through woods and hills. And as time went on, I was able to more easily quiet the incessant thought stream always moving through my head and often constricting my view of the world. This allowed me to incrementally loosen the tight grip and narrow confines of my ego on awareness and to return to the Now, to presence. In presence, without the filtering influences of thought, experience becomes more holistic, immediate, and unbroken. In that state, William Blake's "doors of perception" are cracked open and new possibilities in awareness begin to emerge

Gradually it became possible for me to see and feel the world at a deeper level, in a way that was totally new and fascinating. I was learning to shift into a more perceptive consciousness that enabled me to sense the underlying ocean of energy in which all of existence is rooted. I started to understand that there was a greater Oneness that bound all of everything together as a whole—one energy. I began to see that the ocean and its waves, although they appear separate and distinct, are really one.

As my conditioned belief in being a self separate from everything else became less solid and the distinction between the outside and the inside began to mellow, the larger, unified reality of Oneness opened up. The trees, the rivers, the mountains, sky, rocks, plants, creatures big and small, the rich living smells of the earth, life, and death—it all felt a part of me and me a part of all of it. I was learning how to obtain these shifts naturally, on my own and over time.

I have so many memories with Phoebe when I felt so incredibly alive while engrossed in the ebb and flow of our walks and runs together, as well as in the many moments of stillness. One memory in particular that is alive and clear to this day happened right at twilight.

We were standing on the edge of a cliff looking out over a luxuriantly green river valley buzzing and effervescent with life. As we stood there, it felt as if we were being wrapped and enfolded by the soothing warmth of a deepening summer's dusk. Feelings of mystery and a specter of moist, earthy scents were rising up from the river bottom, suffusing the space in and around us. Phoebe was peering so intently into the living wave of green that she began to tremble with what seemed to be every atom of her body. So accustomed to doing as she would do, I found the same intensity filling me.

In a moment the usual and conditioned sense of "me" dropped and "I" was suddenly, and once again, everywhere and everything —and nothing, nothing in particular that is. I was all of it, all that I sensed, felt, and all that surrounded me. Yet there was no longer a "me" as a separate self; there was nothing but pure experience, spacious awareness. It felt extraordinary and perfectly natural at once. I was unexpectedly overtaken and filled by a love for the limitless mystery of Life—Infinite Life. It was a taste of Oneness sparked by my silent black-and-white Yoda, inexpressible in its depth of effect.

When Phoebe died, she died in my arms. I remember my father and me sobbing uncontrollably. I will never forget that day with him and our gut-wrenching sorrow, but it was a time and sadness that I am so thankful we shared. It was my first real experience of death. Phoebe was part of me because our lives had become so profoundly intertwined as one. I felt lost and hurt in a way I'd never experienced before. I suffered the stabbing pain of something suddenly being ripped out of my body and seemingly lost forever. Tears well in my eyes as I think back on it now.

Death of what is loved deeply is a fall into the very opposite of Oneness. But as life will invariably show us, to know and love something with all one's heart sometimes requires the bitter and painful taste of its opposite. But in that intense contrast of feeling and experience is the higher possibility of moving beyond opposites and into a wiser Oneness.

We buried Phoebe in the rich river silt of our garden. Before burying her, I had a sudden thought to put some physical part of myself with her, so I laid two recently extracted wisdom teeth on top of her before covering her with fresh earth—bone to bone, essence to essence. From Phoebe I learned to listen with every living ounce of my being, to love nature in ways I may not have discovered without her. It was with her that I began to really wake up to the beauty and wonder of Oneness and to feel a sense of the universe's true possibilities and sacredness. And for that I am forever grateful.

Tree Reveler

The stereotype that has grown up around the idea of appreciating trees in a way that might go "against the grain" of what most consider normal or acceptable—being a "tree hugger"—is unfortunate. Perhaps it would be better to start fresh, with an expression free of negative connotations, such as "tree reveler." I would definitely fall into that category, but I am certainly okay with being called a tree hugger too. I unabashedly admit that I have embraced wholeheartedly more than a few trees in my day; sometimes it just feels like the right thing to do. And many of the unity experiences I recollect here took place in settings or situations where trees were present and a vital part of the experience.

Trees are invaluable to the human story—from our very beginnings. I doubt that life, especially human life, would be as it is now without the essential and pivotal role trees have played in shaping our unfolding adventure as a species. We often honor that relationship through our treasured childhood stories about trees, such as the magical story *The Giving Tree* by Shel Silverstein, where we are taught the valuable lessons of life's larger truths expressed through beautiful but simple words and images around the life, death, and selfless giving of a tree.

Most of us have also heard of the "The Tree of Life"—a metaphor common to diverse cultures and spiritual traditions throughout history: The Tree of Life that is a sacred unifying symbol in the Kabbalah, the wisdom tradition of Judaism; or Christianity's Garden of Eden and the Tree of Knowledge with its forbidden fruit of duality; or the Celtic Tree of Life, Crann Bethadh, the link between heaven and earth. These stories and myths with trees at their centers illustrate our deep-rooted connection to both the earth and the cosmos as one. Trees are often used as symbols to point to the ultimate unity of earth and heaven, the conscious and the subconscious, matter and spirit—of the finite and infinity.

For example, we can imagine the creative potential of one seed as it gives rise to the first roots of a new tree, which begin to grow deep and wide in the dark, mysterious depths of the earth, grounding and nourishing it. From that rootedness in the earth emerges the mighty trunk and sacred body of the tree, growing upward and supporting the life force of the tree as it reaches for the unknown expanse of the heavens. The tree flowers and creates more seeds, on and on until the tree dies. It is the perfect symbol of the intertwined, spiraling cycle of life, death, and rebirth. In a similar way, a tree can also symbolize our recognition of the unity that underlies the dual nature of life: While discovering and embodying the groundedness and rootedness of our earthly existence, we can also aspire toward the realization of our higher celestial and spiritual potentials—understanding in the end that they are inseparable.

In the changing landscape of my own life, there are vivid memories of certain special trees. With sweet nostalgia I revere the mighty

Chapter 4–Experiences of Oneness from My Life

oaks of my Florida childhood—rope swings and high-perched tree forts, or the aspen groves of Colorado transforming into a golden fire in the fall, shimmering with luminous greens in the summer. Mixed in with the oaks and aspens are my cherished memories of the blanket of dark-green pine forests of the western states; the majestic, gigantic redwoods of California; the complex weave of countless trees in the rainforests of Central America; the hardwood forests of the eastern US, ablaze with fiery oranges, reds, yellows, and every mix in between.

I have come upon certain trees that have truly reached out and taken hold of my attention. They are trees that shine forth a life presence that is undeniable in its powerful effect—usually older, bigger trees, but not always. If we are open-minded and silently receptive, trees like these can trigger a natural shift into a state of wonder and reverence, similar to the sudden stillness of mind that grand and magnificent landscapes or elemental powers can evoke, but different in that trees are living beings.

A tree is aware not in the way of thought, but a slower, subtler, primordial awareness emerging out of the living vitality of a rooted existence, a beautiful expression of the elemental forces and energies of life given unique form. It sometimes feels to me that trees, because of the rich and complex web of energetic relationships they form, actually create a type of living nervous system for the planet itself, like an electrical fabric of outward facing, earthly neurons.

This is the perfect place to point out that modern science does not exclude unity experiences from the scope of human realization and possibility. To the contrary, scientific knowledge can actually enhance those experiences by helping one develop a stronger connection and more integrated understanding of life from a larger and more inclusive perspective. The key is to use the incredible diversity of knowledge generated though science as a way of ultimately moving toward an increasingly unified experience of Reality, of Life in a big sense—instead of allowing it to continue to create a continually divisive and fragmenting mode of consciousness.

The knowledge then that I carry about the life of trees informs and enables the possibility of a more encompassing sensitivity and perceptiveness. The trick is learning how to consistently disengage that voice of knowledge when needed. It is imperative that once knowledge is gained we also learn to become open to those states of consciousness beyond information, discriminating logic, and the thinking mind's habit of naming and labeling everything.

When I am in the presence of a tree that draws me, as thoughts quiet and slowly drop off, as the habitual defining lines of the ego self begin to dissipate, an expansion of awareness becomes possible. In that opening there arises the feeling of a merging connection and a return to Oneness. It is an experience of a tree in an entirely novel way and at a much profounder level, yet it feels so familiar. To know and relate to trees in this way is to recognize the life energies we all share as living, growing, and dying beings, as individuals and as one. Once again, it is realizing that the many waves that appear separate are in actuality indivisible and whole. It is recognizing the tree for the forest *and* the forest for the tree.

One of the marvels of consciousness is the possibility of knowing a tree in a way that bypasses our projected thoughts or ideas of how we *expect* it to be. Experienced in that way, a tree can be rediscovered in all its original freshness and aliveness—as it is, pure and simple: a perfect expression of the infinite creativity and unity of Life itself.

Gardening the Cosmos

Another doorway into experiences of Oneness is gardening—in any of its many forms. Like so much of our experience of reality, a more comprehensive grasp of one small part or facet of the universe often translates into a better and deeper understanding of the whole. The intricate and interconnected dynamic of gardening from start to finish is a microcosmic doorway into the macrocosmic. The garden is a portal into Life as infinite—through an immersion in and a connection with life in a finite scale. It is a way to participate closely with heart, body, and mind in the tightly interrelating processes and patterns of the cycles of life and cosmos.

In the garden, with hands, senses, awareness, and feeling, we tune in to and participate intimately with the universal rhythms, with life's limitless and inextinguishable energy expressed in countless living forms, seen and unseen. We begin to see the elemental powers of earth, wind, water, moon, and sun along with life's vital force as one spiraling, cycling movement of growth and transformation, light and dark—death out of life, life out of death.

Tended in the garden too is our deeply rooted love of the natural world; it is there that we are able to soak up the sensual richness of the living earth, and we begin to sense in a profounder way the marvel of existence itself, of being alive in this moment. It is a return to the timeless Now, to presence. Yet at the same time, we are also able to appreciate experientially, through feeling, through skin, muscle, and bone, those timebound cycles of nature that give us life.

Added to this is the miraculous generative power of the seed, a mirror in tiny scale of the same creative power that our universe possesses. Through the catalyzing powers of soil, microorganisms, rain, sun power, oxygen, carbon dioxide, and numerous other interacting processes, a single seed transmutes into a seedling, into a growing plant that flowers and fruits, finally creating many seeds from one. Within this circle, the seed's latent life force is brought to fruition; the energy of sun and element is captured and changed into the flesh of a new plant's body, fruits, and seeds. That living energy then becomes our sustenance and nourishment, is transformed into our flesh and blood, becomes our power to heal, grow, and to be self-aware.

In the garden is the possibility of discovering the complex relationships and interdependencies that create the unified web of our lives and that point us to a greater unity—to the infinite seed, source, and ground from which all existence arises.

The garden is also the perfect place for the possibilities of flow, wonder, and the higher peak states to emerge. One side of gardening is about preparing, encouraging, and attempting to work with, or sometimes even enhance nature's own intrinsic intelligence. It took me a while to figure that one out—that I was simply helping a natural process take hold and do its own thing. I wasn't really in control of anything other than taking care of the details of design, timing, and care. But in those moments of making that happen, in the sheer enjoyment of being active in that way, I would sometimes become so wrapped up and engrossed in the sensing and doing that thoughts and self would drop off so that "I" wasn't there anymore; garden, gardener, and gardening become one.

Sometimes it would happen only for a few moments and other times I had no idea how long "I" was gone. And by saying that, I am definitely not referring to spacing out or daydreaming. Instead, it is that same sense that I have alluded to often of being aware in a way that is both intent and focused while still remaining open and expansive. Self boundaries loosen, and the doorway to flow, wonder, and deeper Oneness is opened. If flow is entered, it is a slow flow—the speed of life; it is an active presence and stilled knowing that embodies and fills with the energies of the garden's unfolding—preparing the earth, planting seeds, watering, enriching the soil, supporting, clearing or adding, and encouraging vitality and growth.

The other side of gardening is the more receptive and nonactive, part, a shifting from "doing" to "being." It is a stilled presence that allows us to step back in silent wonder, to sense, feel, and listen with everything. Thoughts remain disengaged and there is the feeling that attention moves from a fixation with thoughts into the wider spaces and awareness beyond our bodies. There have been times when I felt as if I was merging with and becoming a part of all before me and around me: soil, plants, uncountable microorganisms, flowers, fruits, birds, trees, sky, clouds, rain, wind, and sunshine. But the "me" wasn't there anymore, and I knew immediately in those moments and without thinking that I am all of this and more, worldly and infinite at once.

Discovered in these types of unity experiences is Big Life realized as the source and stage for everything, for all of existence. In the garden, if we are quiet and attentive, inside becomes outside, and outside becomes inside—subject and object meld into one and then there is just a profound and heart-centered gratitude, a deep love for this mystery of being here, alive, and aware. And the wonder of it all is that it might happen right here and now in any light-filled garden—while gardening the Cosmos.

Wild Places

What follows are unity experiences brought out by encounters with the self-transcending powers of the earth itself, the magnificent diversity and stunning beauty of its wild places, along with the endless creative expressions and interplay of the elemental forces of earth, wind, water, sun, and the life force. But there are two ecosystems in particular that stand out as absolutely unique in terms of life's amazing capacity to create and nurture an unimaginable richness and variety: coral reefs and rainforests.

Coral Reefs

My first experience with a coral reef was completely unexpected, a surprise and discovery beyond anything I thought possible. When entering a wild space that is overflowing and flourishing with such a profusion and diversity of life, intensely vivid colors, and varied forms, the wonder state is almost instantaneous, automatic. In a sense it is like being shocked into stillness and presence because the scene is so moving, so unanticipated and captivating that there is no space for anything but silent wonder. There is only presence—and a feeling of the impossible becoming possible. Add to this the rhythmic, naturally meditative sounds of inhalations and exhalations resonating through a snorkel or diving regulator and presence finds it anchor.

A marvel-filled quietness happens easily as one is overtaken and totally enthralled by a reef's theater of life: pastel-hued parrotfish, angelfish, multicolored hard and soft corals, dancing schools of snapper, grunts, doctor, and surgeonfish, crabs tiny and large, lobsters, eagle and stingrays, sharks, grouper, a plethora of different sea plants and algae, trumpet and pufferfish, triggerfish, electric-blue wrasses, thousands of silvery minnows, and on and on. Life shines forth everywhere, from every possible space. To experience a healthy coral reef is like being in the middle of a rainbow that has burst into a million gleaming, vibrant, living pieces, but then realizing that all the parts that appear separate and distinct are really interconnected and one.

Presence deepens further with the hypnotic and amplified sound of breathing. Vision becomes clearer and sharpens; colors are more intense and alive. The detail is incomprehensible and that is only what is immediately and directly sensed. The intuited goes much further: the life out there is the life in here—one and the same.

While trying to take in and contain the beautiful complexity of a coral reef there is often a shifting of awareness from the whole to the parts, then back to the larger whole. It is a unified comprehension of the one and the many, joined and indivisible. Again and again the mind empties and returns to the whole, to the rhythms and the dynamic flow of the ocean and its pulsing energy, to the balanced harmony of life, death, and transformation. Hours pass in seconds; time and self disappear. As the world of thought subsides and there is only this miracle of living color, of glimpsing the infinite in the finite, there is a growing understanding that this is who I am in heart and essence.

The idea of the planet's coral reefs dying because of human-caused and -related factors is heartbreaking. I've seen the degradation in places that I have returned to repeatedly over the years, and it saddens me deeply, especially in places where I've worked on education projects with the goal to slow that decline. My genuine hope is that this vision of wholeness and growth of consciousness that I talk about, that is shared by many others, will take root, inspire, and be acted upon—in time to get it right.

The Rainforest

I still travel back to the islands of Bocas del Toro, Panama, where I was a Peace Corps volunteer. I return to maintain those friendships built while I lived and worked there, to see and feel the ocean I love and hold sacred—and for the waves. About three years after leaving the Peace Corps, a girlfriend and I returned to Bocas Island and, with the help of some local friends, had a small rancho built right next to a swath of dense rainforest. I affectionately refer to this tree house-like home as the "jungle bungalow." It was constructed high up on stilts in order to take advantage of the ocean breezes that manage to pass through the surrounding forest. As a crow flies, the open ocean is only a few miles away.

We lived simply: no plumbing, no electricity, no running water—just rain water collected in giant tanks and lanterns for light. There was also a cheap, tin-can stove and oven that ran off a small tank of propane and an old-fashioned, hand-dug outhouse. It was all that was needed or wanted at the time.

Most of the house was built with an open deck, protected by an overhanging roof. There were hammocks hung from the rafters and much time was spent swaying in them listening, smelling, feeling, and peering into and around the huge wall of rainforest that towered only about forty meters away. My primary mode of transportation was a bike with a pull-behind trailer. It was a step above camping and I loved it. Each time I lived there was a powerful jolt, a perfect and reliable way to snap me out of the comfortable complacency that would overcome me back in the States.

As most of us have heard, a rainforest is one of the most biodiverse places on our planet, but it's deceiving because so much of the forest's life is high in the canopy and difficult to see or identify. Plants, trees, orchids, bromeliads, flowers, fruits, fungi, and mosses are so overwhelmingly varied and profuse that it could take lifetimes to get to know them all.

The abundance of animal and bird life is remarkable as well; some I would see or hear often, others I would spy only occasionally: howler, spider, and capuchin monkeys; sloths; anteaters; ruby-, emerald-, and sapphire-colored birds; boas; poison dart frogs; countless parrots and parakeets; iguanas; kinkajous; tropical vipers and tree frogs—and more. Within this sea of green and in the midst of this abundance of life, there was only amazement and a burgeoning reverence for Life's unending creative wisdom.

But it is sundown and nighttime that are my fondest memories: It is the hour when the world begins to shift into the energy of night and a natural door into a subtler perceptiveness opens. At twilight the jungle awakens, humming and thrumming from its living depths. Lying quiet and still in the hammock, swaddled in this living blanket of sounds, vibration, and warmth, I would sometimes feel as if I was opening outward into all that I was experiencing, becoming one with all I was sensing.

The rainforest's humidity was palpably heavy, but it carried in that moistness a tree-enriched and earthy scent that spoke of life olden and wise. Also mixed in with the sounds and thick smells of the jungle, passing undeterred through millions of leaves, arrived the vibrations of pounding, crashing surf. It was strange at first to hear surf thundering in the middle of a jungle, but it was like having a powerful reverberating bass drum as a unifying background to the higher tones of the forest.

At dusk the dense air also brought with it an immense chorus of frogs, the many trills and melodious sounds of numberless nighttime creatures. And from everywhere, the pulsing, buzzing and humming rhythm of millions of insects was heard and felt—a microcosmic reflection of the creative and generative hum and pulsation of the universe itself.

This rising and falling symphony of sounds was a captivating and vibratory delight. It was a surround of sound that sometimes took hold and stilled my thinking mind with the untamable life force that is everywhere at once in the rainforest. In that embrace of enveloping sound, a bigger picture would come to mind and heart—of connectedness and belonging to something way beyond human comprehension. The rainforest's rhythmic waves of sound could at times transport me into a higher plane of feeling and awareness—creating a pathway into a clearer understanding of Oneness.

Taken over by a family of bats, a small ecosystem of jungle insects, as well as a resident boa constrictor (living in the old and rusty oven) helping to keep the bat population in check, the jungle bungalow has been slowly returning to the rainforest over the last several years. It's certainly a balanced ecosystem, but a little too crowded for my tastes.

The Big Wild

I believe wild places—the vast vistas of mountains, canyons, deserts, oceans, plains, wetlands, and forests, and any other wild settings that draw us in and captivate us—make it possible to forget momentarily our small selves. In their grandness and splendor, we transcend the limitations of our day-to-day doings and enter into a more inclusive and larger picture of Life. It is this wildness, in all its incredible, ever-changing forms, that has the unequaled ability to awaken us to a silent reverie, to presence—and to change us for the better.

Think about the dramatic and lasting effect that the massive grandeur of a mountain or mountain range can have on us, the ancient depths of some colossal canyon, or the elementally sculpted sandstone formations of a desert landscape. Such experiences of expansiveness are powerful enough to lift our spirits, to suffuse them with wonder and deeper meanings. In those instances of nature's awesomeness, the "self" is displaced and blown away. The sense of ego is overcome and illuminated instead by an enormous earthen presence and with the sacredness of Life both limitless and finite. Arising in those moments is a deep and direct knowing that earth and what we call self are indivisible and one. In this way, the earth as pure matter and limitless energy speaks and beckons to us through its booming, primordial silence.

And what about the pure exaltation and reverence sparked by peering into the soul-stirring mysteriousness of a star-filled night sky? That feeling of infinity is an ever-present reminder of the greater whole in which we are all inseparably interwoven. To gaze with mind quiet and heart open into that endless reach of darkness, illuminated by billions of shimmering points of star fire, is to touch and respark the inborn appreciation and wonderment that we all possess for the mystery of existence itself—the greatest mystery of all.

Entering into those heavens so incomprehensibly grand and unfathomable, there stirs a certain knowing and memory of greater origins, of Infinity as home. In this spirit-inspiring recollection, Life is seen in its dance with Death, twirling and circling endlessly. In those moments of peering deep into the unknown, we know without words that we belong to this magnificent spiraling dance of transformation and evolution, to that greater Oneness that is overflowing and ripe with possibility—and new beginnings.

Hot Springs—Sacred and Healing

Nestled in the mountains of Colorado is a treasured place for me. It is a natural sanctuary, pure and pristine, barely touched by artificial lights and where the darkness of the night is like nothing I have ever experienced before. Innumerable stars shine and glisten through the untouchable immensity of space as harbingers of a time long past. It is starlight that, although inherently limitless, is held to the limits of time and space. Gratefully, there are also naturally occurring thermal waters here—tucked in a hidden valley far from everything except wide-open vistas. It is a powerful place.

Sensually warm, mineral-enriched waters in glimmering translucent pools allow the body to be held almost weightless, free of encumbering clothing. It is skin, body, heart, and mind directly in touch with and held by earth-heated spring waters near to or slightly above the body's natural temperature, creating the impression of being bodiless. That feeling, along with the surrounding solace of solitude sets the stage for entering into profounder states of awareness, especially after sundown. On occasion I have sat so relaxed and peaceful in these sensuous, spring-fed pools that I began to feel like I was floating free of form, cradled and one with the warm darkness of water, earth, and the enormity of the star-blazed heavens.

Stillness comes easy and presence fills me during these openings. The small being that I am joins with the greater presence of all that is around me—"embodying" everything as One. Looking up and taking in billions of atomic lights, feeling it in my depths, knowing in a bone-deep way that this vital star radiance is the very substance of flesh and blood, organ and muscle; it is the same life-giving power of our sun, the same energy that is the essence of every living cell. Deeper into stillness and I know without a thought that this One energy and awareness is who I am; Love and gratitude pour from this center that is my center. The universe as "me" is shed of its limitations, returns to its infinite origins.

As the night darkens further, dozens of fireflies flash their tiny lights of inner bioluminescence; it is the same energy of our sun transformed, living, and earthbound. This mystery and wonder root inside, move upward and alight. This is Oneness, the Source, enfolding and unfolding, ebbing and flowing, living and dying. But these are simply thoughts, sculpted words used to point to the Great Unknown that is ultimately ungraspable and indefinable. Yet it is a mystery that is always as close as our skin and as touchable as the beating of our hearts.

To end, I would like to say that there have also been countless other smaller encounters with the wilds of the world that have opened me to wonder and Oneness, too many to recount. These subtler experiences happened because I was paying attention enough to have noticed them, and although they may have been less intense overall, they have all had an undeniably enriching effect in my life.

It may have been something as seemingly insignificant as the vibrant, flashing colors of a bird, the play of light on mountains at dusk and dawn, forests and the ocean at night, a single tree, night sounds, sunsets and sunrises, or the unexpected sight of the moon rising huge and glowing fire-orange over the horizon. Or perhaps it was as slight as a smell or a taste that sparked an opening and quiet pondering. I could go on and on.

These are all the individual notes, the smaller waves that express equally well the boundless and oceanic intelligence of the creative Infinity that allows us the precious gift of discovering the possibilities of love and Oneness.

Part Four
Oneness Close to Home

Two Waves Become One

We are sexual beings, whether it's repressed or expressed, explored or unexplored, denied or embraced. We are sexual at every level—energetically, biologically, emotionally, psychologically, and spiritually. Our sex drive and the unbelievably strong urge we have to procreate are hardwired into us, and regardless of whether we celebrate or disdain the push and pull of this ceaseless desire, it influences a large proportion of what we do and what we choose in our lives. For all living beings, sexual energy is the deep-rooted, primordial fire of life. But unique to us, as self-aware humans, is the potential to transcend those purely biological, instinctual desires of sex in order to move into the higher possibilities of sexual union and Oneness.

Like much of what is discussed here, it is rare that an experience is completely black or white, especially experiences that involve the organizational function of our egos and our tendency to separate the world into parts and degrees of experience. That being said, intimacy and sexual experiences, regardless of orientation, gender, or preference, can also be seen to lie along a continuum of awareness and experience: from the more limited, mostly physical experiences at one end (biological- and hormonal-driven lust and sex without love—the beautiful sexual animal in all of us) to the higher, deeper, and more transcendent types of experiences at the other end—deep love, sacred sex, unity, and Oneness experiences. And then there are all the possibilities and combinations in between.

Sexual intimacy is an unparalleled and readily available way of entering into and experiencing Oneness and love with another human being. And as adults, we at least have an inkling of this possibility; we have all most likely touched upon and had some experience (hopefully a positive one) with the closeness, connection, and Oneness to be found in the sexual sphere of life.

Myriad factors, both elusive and obvious, influence the extent to which we are able to reach the deeper levels of intimacy: the amount of presence brought to the experience, attention and intention, the degree of ego involvement, expectations, preferences, negative or positive past experiences, preformed and habitual ideas of how sexuality should feel, look, and be expressed.

On top of that, there are also the many engrained fears, anxieties, and insecurities created around sex, the level of comfort and depth of feeling involved in any given relationship, along with many other multifarious and often nebulous influences. Sexuality and sexual relations can be incredibly complex and seem overwhelming at times. We have piled on so many preconceptions and so much "self" consciousness—ways of thinking that pull us out of the present. When in reality, sexuality is one of the potentially purest, simplest, and most unifying acts in life.

I, like many people, have at times struggled with the hang-ups and excessive self-consciousness of Western sexuality—the repression and presence-killing burden of self-judgment, criticalness, and self-centeredness. But I have also tasted the higher realms of intimacy and it can be truly transcendent and unifying experience.

From my own tastes of sexual unity experiences, I have come to see how the senses are indispensable as an immediate means for reaching a state of less thought and increasing presence. With a steady and fully attentive awareness to all that is felt and sensed in moments of intimacy, a deeper experience unencumbered by the thinking, judging mind becomes possible. Sight, sound, feeling, taste, and smell become doorways to Oneness. What is normally interpreted as separate feelings and perceptions becomes one sense, like a single highly sensitive, ultra-perceptive super sense.

Here are some of the ways the sensual and unifying powers of our senses might be experienced:

Through sight we are powerfully and magnetically attracted to the body's array of beautiful and enticing colors and forms. We marvel heatedly in its arousing shapes, symmetry, and textures, its warming and exciting curves and lines. The stirring appeal of the skin draws us to touch, feel, and caress its sensual mysteries. We explore with our eyes the softness and hardness of chest, the strength and contour of shoulders, the inviting allure of neck and ears. We relish the captivating roundedness of breasts, the titillating contrasts of lights and darks, of areolas and nipples. We follow and drink in with our eyes the sinuous flow of the spine, provocative lips, and passion-filled faces.

Our eyes shine in anticipation at the sight of an aroused, engorged masculine hardness or the moist, soft pinks and flower-like layers of the feminine. We watch as legs, torsos, and arms intertwine, explore, feel, and move closer and closer to union. In these encounters there is a visual devouring, a sheer delight, and a fire of desire that is ignited and soaked up through the eyes.

Further still, a profounder intimacy can be realized by gazing silently into a lover's eyes, when there is a willingness to be vulnerable, to surrender, and to be open to the greater love and Oneness that lie beyond those openings into our deepest being. It takes tremendous courage to peer directly into the heart and soul of another human being or to have another look into you. But it is through these sight-bestowing windows into the timeless that we are able to glimpse the beauty of higher love and Oneness.

Then there are the audible aspects of lovemaking, all the sounds that excite and arouse us. Entering our ears are the waves of rising and falling breath, soft and easy at first but soon building, mounting, crescendoing, and then softening again. To feel those vibratory vocalizations of pleasure—the gasps, the moans, the untamable whispers of heated passion, and the sometimes unstoppable screams of intense and unexpected pleasure—stirs and lights our passion like nothing else. To hear the sweet and erotic sounds of bodies joining and moving into and out of a shared silky wetness is pure, unbridled ecstasy. It is an ecstatic fusion and Oneness born out of the rising sounds, the silences, and intense blending of lust and love. If one is able to sense with one's whole being and without thought or expectation, this wordless language of love, the door to true union, to the fire of heart and spirit, is opened.

Smell and taste also possess the undeniable ability to generate a growing ardor and a sense of merging one into the other. The mouthwatering scents and tastes of sex, of impassioned desire and love are lively, varied, and deliciously arousing. And as most of us know, the gustatory and olfactory go hand in hand, each accentuating the other. As bodies are stoked in heated embrace, the bodily waters of intensifying intimacy and connection begin to flow freely, intermingling and growing stronger in effect and appeal. Inhaling and soaking up the sensual fragrance of a lover is powerful in such an incredibly affecting way.

The masculine and feminine energies of each body mix, transform, and become a stirring synergy. Invisible, powerful pheromones rise and fill the air with their irresistible influence. A warm moistness covers us, carrying titillating aromas and flavors from every nook, exciting the depths of body, mind, and heart. The scent and taste of bodies in union combine the sweet and slight tanginess of earth with the saltiness of sweat and ocean, all coming together in erotic Oneness.

Bring in the carnal and unifying sensations aroused by the feeling of skin touching skin, warm silky flesh against flesh, hardness entering and embraced by softness, and the gateway to Oneness opens even more. With heart to heart, the outer joining and fusing with the inner, the separation and the boundaries defined by our skin and bodily form, that normally feel so definite and sure, begin to grow transparent as a deeper intimacy takes hold. There is a breaking through, a letting go wholly into the pure pleasure and sensuality of touch, of closeness, and togetherness. Where there were once two bodies that distinction begins to blur, and there is an intensifying sense of growing Oneness. The usual solid feeling of being an individual begins to lose its concreteness; where does one body stop and the other begin? The answer becomes uncertain as new possibilities of Oneness open up.

The heart, along with the deeper emotions that pour forth during intimate unity experiences, can move us even further into Oneness. As the sharing of love heightens, there is a growing feeling that all senses and sensations are fusing and no longer separate. Flowing in, through, and out of the heart is an upwelling of love that is transformed into the experience of a powerfully felt Oneness. The mind too, without thought, knows this Oneness of love and helps bring it to fruition through an opening of our intuitive intelligence and understanding of the sacredness of sexual union.

Sex without love can never reach or obtain the same heights or depths as with it. Love is the grand unifier and in its highest form is Oneness. Sexual intimacy and union are the ultimate expressions of that higher love, when lover and beloved become One, when two bodies, two seemingly separate selves are momentarily transcended, wrapped in the arms of the other.

By far one of the greatest pleasures and mysteries in life is the human orgasm. It can be one of the most joyfully intense, "uncontrolled" letting-go experiences we ever feel. At its peak, the orgasmic experience is a total loss of control and a rapturous surrender to a flash of Oneness below the surface. In that climaxing moment, we are suddenly emptied of our "selves" and filled with an ecstasy that stops our minds and opens our hearts to true union. And it is not only the joy of the orgasm itself; it's the whole experience—before, during, and after, all of it coming together as one.

Some of my most vivid sexual unity experiences have been tasted in the afterglow moments, when there is a complete, unrestrained relaxing and melding into the other. It is the possibility of two waves clearing and discovering Oneness together. The French call the orgasm "little death," which is true in that it is a heavenly and all-too-short "loss" of self. I think it could also be called "flash of Oneness."

The key is not to let the orgasm become an obsession or an end in itself, losing presence and enjoyment of all that comes before and after. The deeper experiences of sexual union can only occur in presence, in our capacity to be fully in the moment, in love and at one with another human being. These possibilities of intimate Oneness open up when we are able to disengage and free ourselves from the contracting fears that arise out of our often unrelenting thoughts about the past and future. Then there is return to the Now, to a presence that is filled with a balance of the erotic energies and fiery passions of the body blended in harmony with the unifying, deeper love of the heart.

In those sacred moments, bodies join, merge, and become one in that timeless, boundless dimension of deep joy that is discovered in the being of another, in the possible creation of one life from two—when two waves become one. In this circular, sensual dance of separateness and Oneness, we uncover and partake consciously in the creative cosmic patterns that mirror perfectly the universal rhythms at the heart of our shared beings.

Rhythmic Union—Music and Dance

Music and dance are undeniable treasures of human existence; they are pure and authentic reflections of the vibratory, energetic, and creative powers of the universe itself. Music has the ability to free us, to open us to that Source of deeper harmony and Oneness that is the resonant heart of all that is, and to reunite us with the possibilities underneath our thinking minds.

In dance we celebrate Life's universal rhythms given expression through music. In fact, in many of the unity experiences recounted here, I use the word "dance" as a way to convey those feelings of ecstatic joy revealed in experiences of Oneness. Music as defined by Merriam-Webster's dictionary is "the science or art of ordering tones or sounds in succession, in combination, and in temporal relationships to produce a composition having unity and continuity." It is energy given form through sound ultimately creating feelings of beauty and stirring emotion.

In a sense, music is a universal language, a type of cosmic mathematics bestowed with the powers of rhythm, melody, harmony, sound, and evolution. All of these elements unfold in unison to continuously inform the universe with organized, symmetrical, and meaningful patterns of energy, creation, and awareness. They enrich existence with beauty, form, and function.

The musical essence and ground of our universe is an ordered and ever-evolving "symphonic" dance of vibratory, pulsating energy, alternating beats of potentiated emptiness and of creative fullness, between possibility and actuality, creation and destruction, life and death. In this way music is a mirror of the universe's endless capacity for novelty and creativity. And finally, music and dance are unmatched doorways into states of Oneness, into flow, wonder, and high peak experiences.

I can think of many occasions when music and dance allowed me to "lose my'self'," "to get lost in the beat," to be pulled in, lifted up, and wholly surrendered to the melody, the pulse and flow, and the rhythmic story being told. And I believe it's safe to say that most people have had similar experiences. In those moments, our normally isolated sense of self-awareness opens up to move in harmony with something bigger than our small selves; we are irresistibly urged and drawn to dance; to twirl, jump, and gyrate; to groove in time with the alluring beat. Through the energy and flow of dance and music is the possibility to feel unbelievably alive.

As the boundaries of self are gradually loosened by the irresistible energy of the music, a sense of the boundlessness takes hold, separateness begins to dissolve; music and musician, music and listener, dance, song, and dancers all become one. In that state I have been able to dance tirelessly for hours and it seemed like minutes, and the person or people danced with felt closer than before—without saying a word.

The type of music and whether one is playing it or simply listening make no difference; that part is more of a preference or a passion. As usual though, presence is the key, and music encourages the possibility of presence better than almost anything. Music and dance have an unsurpassed ability to help us still our minds, expand awareness, and return to the Now. Knowing this, it then becomes a matter of letting go of control and surrendering to the inherent power of the rhythm and melody that helps us to disengage our thinking minds and rejoin the spontaneity of the moment.

Percussion instruments in particular lend themselves to this movement toward presence and the opening of our minds. We all know the power of the drum in our bones, passed on from all those before us who also danced in whirling circles and lost themselves in the beat.

These days I can pick up my guitar, start playing without any preset ideas or songs in mind, and frequently move into flow and other degrees of Oneness with relative ease and consistency. The melody, the changing sequence of chords, the tempo—it all just happens—no words, no singing, just the flowing music and knowing without thinking what works. Sometimes when my guitar is just sitting there I swear it feels like it contains and emanates those feelings and states I've discovered through it, and it draws me back for more.

Although many music-inspired unity experiences occur as solitary events or shared with only a few, there is no denying the potential to be discovered in a collective unity experience as well. When thousands of people are involved and present, the shared human energy that can be generated during charged musical performance has the power to melt separation like nothing else. Unified musical experiences like that can erase the habitual perception of separateness and difference across all the usual boundaries—sexual, racial, cultural, political, religious, and national.

Think of the far-reaching, positive effects Bob Marley's reggae music has had on the world. I have heard his songs being played in the jungle, on beaches far and wide, in crowded cities, and in the middle of nowhere. People everywhere know and appreciate his simple message of solidarity and Oneness. That is the potential and larger unifying power of music—transforming and unforgettable to say the least. But it is often the exception rather than the rule. A lot has to go right and fall into place for the collective unity experience to ignite, catch, and burn brightly and continuously: timing, setting, energy levels, moods, and chemistry—of both the audience and the musicians.

When the magic does happen, when the spark catches, it can be staggering. It is as if thousands of individuals have become one being, like thousands of waves becoming one unstoppable wave of energy, force, emotion, and joy—a tsunami of unitive power and feeling. In this united experience a greater Oneness is revealed; love and gratitude flow and pour forth exponentially. The power of a collective human energy directed toward Oneness, toward goodness, higher truth, and beauty is atomic. Connecting to a musician or musicians who are in a state or flow or deeper is to know and experience music, musician, and audience as one, when the music plays itself like never before. And that is music's incredible ability: to create a bridge to Oneness and a way to carry feelings of wonder, love, and thankfulness into the vastness.

Here is a quote from a profoundly wise and thought-provoking book by Duane Elgin called *The Living Universe*. These words say it all:

"The world looks solid and concrete but upon closer inspection solidity breaks down, and material reality becomes a vast ocean of vibrations, frequencies, and harmonies that converge, moment by moment, to produce the stable reality around us. Everything that exists—from atoms to humans to galaxies—has its 'song-line' or unique orchestration that contributes to the whole. We are made from music. To say we are a body of music isn't just poetic; it is also true."

Art and Artist, Two yet One

Art, like music and dance, arises out of that pressing, often untapped desire to use our imaginations to create something novel and beautiful; we all have the potential to be artistic in some way and at some level. The way those artistic possibilities are given expression is open; the forms are many. And as with other unity experiences, it is ultimately our state of mind and our intention to be fully attentive to the present moment that matters most. The creative process, if allowed to unfold naturally, without being forced or distorted by thoughts of how it "ought to be," is an excellent pathway to internal stillness and Oneness. With our totalities being focused on the creative act before us, awareness is unchained from the limits of thought; we are then able to plug into the greater creativity of unity consciousness—when the right brain and the left brain have joined forces. Art is a reflection of the power of human consciousness to uncover and partake directly in the universal creative dynamic, to discover and express wholeness from a palette of endless particulars and to create what has never been seen before.

With any artistic endeavor, if there are thoughts or ideas of failure, fears, and preconceptions that it won't be good enough, it will remain only an ego-centered activity, restrained by those doubts and learned insecurities. The trick is remembering to disengage our thinking, sometimes overly critical minds by learning to act spontaneously and intuitively; it is being able to enter our imaginations into the moment, letting go of how we have been taught to believe art should be. The beauty of art is that what we think are mistakes can often be transformed into its best parts: those serendipitous moments when an accidental line, mark, drop of paint, or awkward form becomes beautiful. My love of art began in earnest when I finally gained that wisdom.

I have discovered the joy of the artistic flow mostly through the mediums of clay and paper—sculpture, drawing, and doodling. Ideally, whatever comes up, I allow to rise unimpeded by thought; I become open to and give form to those images, intuitions, and urges that emerge without judgment: form and color, dark and light, emptiness, geometry, depth and dimension, lines and points. In the midst of creative moments, sometimes hidden patterns and larger meanings emerge—the particular and the universal, the immanent and transcendent, the background and the foreground, shadow and solidity. All are incorporated in both a metaphorical and literal sense. The creative moment is realized most easily in and through the power of our silence and our willingness to let go and let happen.

On the other hand, the receptive side of art is the wonder state: the unsurpassed enjoyment of beauty in and of itself, simply finding a moving pleasure in the aesthetic possibilities of life through art created by others, with all the senses and with heart and mind. The most affecting experiences for me have been when I have been able to find enough presence to enter into the consciousness and energy of another human's creativity. When an art form is encountered and felt directly, when it resonates immediately and bodily with some deeper truth in us, that can be the opening into Oneness. It is a moment when the mind quiets spontaneously while still responding with one's totality: bodily, emotionally, intuitively, and soulfully, to an experience of another's creative energies—instead of through the superimposed medium and interpretation of words.

Regardless of how it is interpreted by an individual or culturally, beautiful art can be a direct pathway to the transcendent, to the sublime, and to Oneness. We can enter those states even while appreciating and understanding in more depth the "parts" that compose and articulate the beauty and truth of the whole. The greater truths discovered through art are visceral experiences that shift awareness both inward and outward simultaneously—rejoining the inner and outer. Through art we are able to move outside our small selves and expand into larger and more creative relationships with the world.

> "Art enables us to find ourselves and to lose ourselves
> at the same time."
> —Thomas Merton, *No Man Is an Island*

Oneness Revealed in Life's Paths

Genuinely open-hearted and sincere service to others can also be an avenue to self-forgetting and unity experiences. Open-hearted awareness is consciousness that has grown beyond self-centeredness and has become relatively free of a primary focus on external gains or rewards. We all have to make a living, but we can change our attitudes and beliefs in relation to "how" we make that living. Do we create and follow a vision of service to the world that is rooted in a desire for the greater good for all, and for the health of the planet in which our lives are 100 percent dependent? Or do we take a job because it's the most convenient, easiest, and best-paying option at the time, unconcerned about or oblivious to long-term repercussions? We'll do what we love and what is best for the larger whole later. I've certainly made both choices over the years.

The late Joseph Campbell, a famous mythologist and prolific writer of our time, offered the sage advice that we "follow our bliss" in life. What he was suggesting is that each of us must explore, discover, and create a genuinely meaningful and fulfilling path in life by listening to and following our deeper callings—not anyone else's or society's. The word "bliss" might be easy to misconstrue here. Campbell was not referring to living a careless, ego-centered, narcissistic, or hedonistic life of wild abandon and endless selfish pleasures. He was instead pointing to the possibility of an empowered life lived with authenticity, integrity, and the deep joy discovered in following our heart's path—for the benefit of the individual and the whole.

The consequence of not following our heart's deeper desires is to live in what he called the "wasteland": a life deprived of true happiness, meaning, and satisfaction. To Campbell the wasteland meant giving in to the grind and the inevitable pull of the rat race by mindlessly becoming one of the herd, letting the choice of life's path happen based mostly or entirely on the ability to make money easily and quickly, or by simply doing what others say is the "right" thing to do.

Unfortunately, there is, of course, the other half of that story, often in stark contrast to this idealized notion of finding and realizing one's true calling. There are times when you just have to take whatever work you can find; life's monetary pressures, all the bills and debt common to contemporary life don't just wait around for the perfect situation to appear. I can personally attest to that reality having spent years working in jobs that I detested, changing them often. It took me a while to finally figure it out, to see that I could create happiness in whatever occupation I was involved in as long as it wasn't detrimental to me or others.

As we all hopefully find out sooner rather than later, no job is perfect, including the perfect ones (that may be a bumper sticker somewhere). Eventually we also figure out that all the money, stuff, vacations, and accomplishments that we accumulate and work so hard for usually lose their shine after a while—especially if they are not rooted in a bigger picture of Oneness, larger meanings, and compassion.

What it took for me to change was to finally embrace the all-too-easy-to-forget wisdom that I am ultimately the one responsible for how I experience the world, regardless of the situation or external circumstances. For each of us that is our power. It is the power of choice—to decide how what is happening is experienced. Do I "react" mindlessly and out of habit or do I "respond" with vision and deliberate intention? It's crazy to me how many times I thought it was just easier to complain and suffer, to find excuses. As I slowly learned to listen more closely and pay attention to my own natural talents and inclinations, I was eventually drawn to the fields of teaching and nursing—and later writing.

The Nurse

For the last eight years I have been working as a registered nurse, and it has been a major mind opener for me in so many unexpected ways. It is a profession that requires learning how to care for people when they are often at their most vulnerable, when they are overwhelmed with fear, anxiety, and uncertainty; disoriented by pain, drugs, and discomfort; and usually in dire need of a little genuine care and empathy. Having worked as a critical care nurse in an intensive care and burn unit, I have seen unimaginable suffering, real hell on earth: patients slowly dying from bone-exposed bedsores—festering and impervious to antibiotics, sickly yellow skin and eyes, fire scorched, blistered and blackened bodies, huge bloated stomachs, failing organs, cancer-eaten lungs and intestines, unstoppable infections, pain, and misery so intense that it was only relieved by drug-induced unconsciousness.

I have also experienced death up close and personal and have shared with family members the unbearable pain of loss. Sickness that brings us near or right to the edge of death can be that final wake-up call. In truth, at death's doorstep it becomes more like a yell, a scream to finally see and appreciate the preciousness and fragility of life, to at last recognize what matters most in life—not the accumulation of wealth and show, not the sense of security we so carefully build or the job, the roles, and labels we cling to so tenaciously; those things all quickly fall or are torn away. Instead, close to the edge, we hopefully see and feel with renewed clarity the truth of what really matters: health, the incredible possibilities of our particular lives, the love, Oneness, and the presence of family, friends, and the countless others who touch us, make our lives meaningful, fulfilling, and whole.

If we let it, if we listen and allow the wisdom of our mortality to speak to us, unbelievable transformations can happen. I have witnessed some of the most miraculous recoveries imaginable, experiences that spoke to me of the incredible enduring and healing power of the human body, mind, heart, and spirit. It is through those experiences that I have been enabled to peer deep into the essence of what it means to be human and to know in my heart that it is this "being" that makes us "human beings"—and one.

Over the years that feeling of Oneness has become clearer to me as I have learned to be more present with people in general. Those changes in attention and awareness that presence fosters have had a tremendous impact in the way I have been able to relate to my patients and to gain their trust. To be fully present with another, to remain empathetic in a way that avoids overly identifying with or judging their particular situations or their pain and suffering, to me is the very heart of compassionate presence.

To be truly present with and to connect with another is to get beyond and outside of the limiting ego-centered self in a way that knows without question that the suffering of another person is my suffering, that this self and this person I call other are one and the same being—regardless of skin color, beliefs, culture, whether rich or poor, mean-spirited or kind, obese or fit. That is when care for another human arises and is given naturally, unconditionally, and without thought. It just happens and flows in the best way possible, for all involved. That is when Oneness and love are known and acted upon from a higher and wider consciousness.

Understanding and regaining the power of presence has certainly involved some growing pains, but happily it has become a more consistent state of mind and base of action for me these days. Clearly, some days are still better than others. I can say without reserve though that any nurse who has been a nurse for long enough and who still finds meaning and enjoyment in their profession will have stories and know in their depths those feeling of Oneness, compassion, and connectedness that I have been talking about. Those are the nurses you want on your side. Anyone who has ever spent enough time in a hospital, as a patient or with family or friends, will likely recognize right off and appreciate the unequaled value of having a nurse who works, lives, and gives with a heart of compassionate presence. The difference is undeniable.

The Teacher

For several years before becoming a nurse, I taught marine and coral reef-based environmental education in the Peace Corps and then was a naturalist and science teacher after that. Teaching, too, can have its inspired moments when the teacher and those taught move into a more unified space of awareness. They are those times when the teachings flow effortlessly between all involved. A connection is made, a sharing of energy, of information and knowledge happens that seems direct and clear, like being plugged in and downloaded with new information almost instantly.

Attention is at a peak, silently absorbing with rapt fascination all that is coming in through the senses and intuition like a sponge, ready for more. Words, images, feelings, new concepts, and interrelationships are soaked up and assimilating without the interference of our normally divisive ways of thinking and categorizing information. Instead, teacher and learner become united conduits and receivers for a transmission and an understanding that feels to be complete, at once and whole. It is as if the knowledge is already there somehow, it just has to be recalled and integrated. In a learning environment like that, when the flow and wonder states have come into play, the space becomes charged with the excited feelings of discovery. Curiosity is ignited.

On occasion as a teacher, I have had flow and wonder experiences like the above, but more often it has been the case that I was on the receiving end. There are those rare professors or teachers who are consistently able to get into the groove of flow and possess the uncanny capacity to regularly spark the wonder state in others. Teachers with that kind of skill are usually so impassioned and enthusiastic about what they are teaching, are still open-minded learners themselves, and know their topic so well, that the flow and wonder states often unfold with ease—and become contagious. These extraordinary teachers know how to create an inspiring freshness and exciting aliveness every time they teach.

I remember one philosophy professor who would come into class on fire, ready to light everyone else's. He was teaching Eastern and Western mysticism and sometimes he actually seemed possessed by the mystics of the past, tapping their wisdom and passing it on to us. That class was over in minutes.

In the end, any occupation or path in life, as long as it isn't inherently and intentionally negative or unnaturally harmful in some way to people, life, ecosystems, or the planet, has the potential of becoming a pathway from a consciousness of isolated, meaningless parts and fragments to one of greater and greater wholeness and meaning, from a separative consciousness to a unitive one.

Walking to Oneness

I end my personal stories of Oneness with what has become the backbone for me for remembering and returning to presence. Almost every day for the last four years or so, regardless of the weather or mood, I go for a walk in the nearby Colorado foothills. It is the same trail that I return to again and again because this particular path has grown to be such an invaluable and loved part of my own waking-up process. It has become a trigger, creating an almost instant shift into groundedness, into a sense of Oneness and expanded awareness.

Along its way is a natural sanctuary exuding and reflecting the energies of a space that is sacred to me. I know this path so well that I recognize when something has changed, when a rock has shifted, if a plant has become sick or has flowered; I know like family the many types of wildlife, plant life, insect life, birds, bushes, and trees that live there, how their habits and appearances transform with the seasons. I never grow tired of its companion-like familiarity; there is a freshness and newness each time I return, and I've returned hundreds of times.

In the past I most probably would have become bored with walking the same trail so frequently. But what I have finally come to understand is that the only boredom in our lives is the state of mind that comes from thinking and being identified with the same old, repeating thought patterns played over and over again. When we learn to become still, meditative, and present, we eventually see that the world always arises fresh and new in each moment; it is never the same. As the Greek philosopher Heraclitus said, "We never step into the same river twice." It is only the thoughts that we habitually and often mindlessly project over reality that cause boredom and prevent us from connecting with the living presence and unity underneath.

The moment I set foot on this beloved rocky trail a change begins to occur. It has become a ceremony of sorts, and there is a power and energy to be harnessed in ritualistic acts when they are enacted with intention and immediacy. As I begin to hike upward, my breathing deepens naturally and my attention moves out of the confines of my head and into the rhythmic cadence of the breath that is entering, filling, and leaving my lungs. I feel in my chest the rising resonance of my beating heart. There is an automatic tuning of all of my senses to the surroundings, an extension of awareness as it expands into the greater sea of energy in which it is immersed. The presence obscured by the usual push and pull of daily living returns.

These meditative walks are in essence the culmination and matured expression of all the other unity experiences I have described, and of the presence I have learned to bring back into my life. Now though, instead of that state of Oneness, of love and nowfulness dissipating as the experience fades, it remains with me, continues, and becomes more of a constant. I have gradually learned to maintain that unified consciousness for longer periods of time, not by controlling anything, but by letting it happen without thinking about or analyzing it. It is the beginning of unitive consciousness becoming rooted and primary instead of secondary.

I will share one more unity experience: walking to Oneness. This happened one evening after hiking to the top of this same trail. There is an opening where I sit to take in the vista of mountains to the west and a long, narrow reservoir that lies rippling, dark gray and silvery below. This is from a journal entry.

On the ridge I sit to go deeper into the stillness that comes spontaneously with the walk up. As the mind noise eases and the concerns of the day let up, thoughts are easily suspended and a widening, energizing awareness takes over. I sit down, release, and let go within the beauty and wonder of the twilight unfolding before me. A bright sliver of luminescent moon slowly ascends above the western horizon, over the lake and the shadowy, looming foothills in the distance. A breeze blows and stirs invisibly through the late summer foliage, whispering in ancient tones of a mystery beyond space and time. Crickets are in full song, in tune and time with the softening colors of the receding day, welcoming the melding powers of the night. I am sitting on the same slanted, flat rocks I have sat on for years. The rocks on which I perch and everything around them are close to me, have shared and been the root of countless hours of reflection, deep silence, and mind-opening insights.

As I let go, as thoughts come and go and gradually fade, I direct my awareness through intention to follow my breath into my body, to feel and fill every atom of flesh and bone, every electrical impulse, every drop of blood and every cell with attention. My whole body feels as if it has begun to breathe and open up, moving out of the smallness of the thinking mind, out of the head and into the larger space of my heart and what is around me—open-hearted awareness.

Awareness in this way is felt and experienced as a continuum, opening into the entire body and beyond. In the growing silence, presence returns; I become both grounded and expansive. A gradual shift is perceived as the usual border between inner and outer begins to feel less solid. The distinction of "I" as "in here" and the world "out there" mellows and relaxes; the usual lines of separation become less defined. All that remains is this precious, unrepeatable moment, an immense and mysterious ocean of energy, and this being that I am—one with the ineffable vastness that is my home and love.

This next chapter is a short collection of other people's lived experiences of Oneness. It is a wisdom that can be, and has been for me, an invaluable guiding light to the deeper wholeness and meaning underneath the separation and disconnect that sometimes cloud our waking lives.

Chapter 5
Oneness as Understood and Experienced by Others

The quotes shared here were collected from a variety of perspectives, time frames, and circumstances. Despite the differences, unity experiences and the many ways of understanding and relating to those experiences finally and inevitably speak to the same Oneness.

Tom Robbins, *Tibetan Peach Pie [A Memoir]*
I suddenly understood everything.
Everything! I saw how the universe worked, how it was put together—on every level, macrocosmic and microcosmic. For as long as it lasted, and it was over I'm guessing in a dozen seconds (in that state time was elastic/geologic), I was witness to an indissolvable totality of reality, a gestalt which normally our monkey minds split into convenient fragments. The rigid fetters that bind us to simplistic dispositions, absurd rationalizations, self-destructive ideologies, and divisive worldviews were severed and I was a free spirit in the oneness of the whole enchilada, seeing the world—material and immaterial— for the all-inclusive miracle it is: not a continuous undifferentiated

glob of stuff, mind you, but more like a great spiraling web whose interconnected threads are beaded with pulsing blips that as much as anything else resemble notes of music. I'm all too aware of how woo-woo this sounds, but it was as real as a stubbed toe and as lucid as a page of Hemingway.

Duane Elgin, *The Living Universe*

The unity of existence is not an experience to be created; rather, it is an always-manifesting condition waiting to be appreciated and welcomed into awareness. The "power of Now" derives from the fact that the entire universe arises in the now as an extremely precise flow. When we are in the Now, we are riding the wave of continuous creation. Each moment is a fresh formation of the universe, emerging [as an unbroken whole] seamlessly and flawlessly.

And

Discovering that we are an inseparable part of the fabric of existence awakens our experience of compassion for the rest of life. We expand our empathy as we come to see ourselves as beings of cosmic dimension and participation. The compassion we feel becomes the basis for a higher unity that transcends our great diversity—racial, ethnic, sexual, generational, religious, political, economic, and more.

Alan Watts, *The Wisdom of Insecurity*

Almost every spiritual tradition recognizes that a point comes when two things must happen: man must surrender his separate-feeling "I," and must face the fact that he cannot know, that is, define the ultimate.

This vision is, then, awareness of this undefinable "something" which we call life, present reality, the great stream, the eternal now—an awareness without the sense of separation from it.

Further

The sense of unity with the "All" is not, however, a nebulous state of mind, a sort of trance, in which all form and distinction is abolished, as if man and the universe merged into a luminous mist of pale mauve. Just as process and form, energy and matter, myself and experience, are names for, and ways of looking at, the same thing—so one and many, unity and multiplicity, identity and difference, are not mutually exclusive opposites: they are each other.

Alan Watts, *The Book*
Under such conditioning [an unquestioned belief in a separate "I"], it seems impossible and even absurd to realize that myself does not reside in the drop, but in the whole surge of energy which ranges from galaxies to the nuclear fields in my body. At this level of existence "I" am immeasurably old; my forms are infinite and their comings and goings are simply the pulses or vibrations of a single and eternal flow of energy.

Joseph Campbell, *A Joseph Campbell Companion*
God is not an illusion, but a symbol pointing beyond itself to the realization of the mystery of at-one-ment.

Charlotte Joko Beck, *Everyday Zen*
[This passage expresses the ability to see beyond self and separation into the unity of pure experience or awareness before thought and form.]
Who we are has many faces, but these faces are not who we are....
Instead of a separate observer [an "I" or a "me"], we should say there is just *observing*. There is no one that hears, there is just hearing. There is no one that sees, there is just seeing.
[If we stick with a meditation practice long enough we eventually see through the faces or coverings of self into our true natures,

when the small self is finally dropped and we view the world from a bigger awareness.]

When nothing sees nothing, what do we have? Just the wonder of life. There is no one who is separated from anything. There is just life living itself: hearing, touching, seeing, smelling, thinking. That is the state of love or compassion: not "It is I," but "It is Thou."

[That is Oneness.]

Lucy Oliver, *The Meditator's Guidebook*

But that brief space when it seemed "you" were not there, and only the world was, has fed something, rejuvenated a nameless part in a way that makes the day worthwhile and slightly wonderful. "You" were present doing the watching, but as an objective observer, part of, yet apart from, that observed. All the trappings of your personality and personal view, which normally interpose between that which sees and that which is seen, had somehow dropped away. Suddenly a more essential You, different from your personality, was seeing, and essence beheld essence.

[In this moment consciousness recognizes consciousness before thought and the self-concept come into play.]

Zen Master Hongzhi, quoted in Thomas Cleary, *Zen Essence: The Science of Freedom*

Zen Mind

Just wash away the dust and dirt of subjective thoughts immediately. When the dust and dirt are washed away, your mind is open, shining brightly, without boundaries, without center or extremes. Completely whole, radiant with light, it shines through the universe, cutting through past, present, and future.

This is inherent in you, and does not come from outside. This is called the state of true reality. One who has experienced this can enter into all sorts of situations in response to all sorts of possibilities, with subtle function that is marvelously effective and naturally uninhibited.

Ken Keyes Jr., *Handbook to Higher Consciousness*

As water evaporates, it becomes transparent vapor. Similarly, at the highest level of consciousness, the experience of "self" becomes transparent vapor that does not affect perception or dam up the intuitive wisdom that is within each of us. As our perception of "self" or "somebody" disappears, we become "nobody"—which then lets us be in a unitive space with everybody.

Ken Wilber, *The Eye of Spirit*

At that point, it becomes obvious that you are not "in here" looking at the world "out there," because that duality has simply collapsed into your pure Presence and spontaneous luminosity.

This realization may take many forms. A simple one is something like this: You might be looking at a mountain, and you have relaxed into the effortlessness of your own present awareness, and then suddenly the mountain is all, you are nothing. Your separate-self sense is suddenly and totally gone, and there is simply everything that is arising moment to moment. You are perfectly aware, perfectly conscious, everything seems completely normal, except you are nowhere to be found. You are not on this side of your face looking at the mountain out there; you simply are the mountain, you are the sky, you are the clouds, you are everything . . .

Moreover, once you glimpse that state—what the Buddhists call One Taste . . . —it becomes obvious that you are not entering this state, but rather, it is a state that in some profound and mysterious way, has always been your primordial condition from time immemorial. You have, in fact, never left this state for a second.

Walter Truett Anderson, *The Next Enlightenment*

[A unity experience shared by a woman who had been going through trying life changes.]

The one [unity experience] I think the most significant and really pivotal happened one night when I was chopping vegetables. I happened to look out the window and I watched a blue jay just through swallowing some water. Time stood still and I saw into the heart of things. I experienced a golden glow and a presence of such great magnitude that nothing in my life prepared me for what I experienced. I understood in those moments that this living presence is everywhere and everything, indivisible and beyond measure. Birth and death, time and space do not apply. The experience of it was boundless love and the knowledge that there is nothing that "is not" this. The somatic experience was like being crushed by love. I felt like a glass vessel holding something I couldn't possibly hold, and about to break.

Sam Harris, *Waking Up*

[This experience occurred while he was visiting an area around the Sea of Galilee, once believed to be frequented by Jesus.]

As I gazed at the surrounding hills, a feeling of peace came over me. It soon grew to blissful stillness that silenced my thoughts. In an instant, the sense of being a separate self—an "I" or a "me"—vanished. Everything was as it had been—the cloudless sky, the brown hills sloping to an inland sea, the pilgrims clutching their bottles of water—but I no longer felt separate from the scene, peering out at the world from behind my eyes. Only the world remained.

Eckhart Tolle, *A New Earth*

There are three words that convey the secret of the art of living, the secret of all success and happiness: "One With Life." Being one with life is being one with the Now. You then realize that you don't live your life, but life lives you. Life is the dancer, and you are the dance. The present moment is the field on which the game of life happens. It cannot happen anywhere else.

Shunryu Suzuki, *Zen Mind, Beginner's Mind*

Before we were born we had no feeling; we were one with the universe. This is called . . . "big mind." After we are separated by birth from this oneness, as the water falling from the waterfall is separated by the wind and rocks, then we have feeling [we become self-aware]. You have difficulty because you have feeling. You attach to the feeling you have without knowing just how this kind of feeling is created. When you do not realize that you are one with the river, or one with the universe, you have fear. Whether it is separated into drops or not, water is water. Our life and death are the same thing. When we realize that fact we have no fear of death anymore, and we have no actual difficulty with our life.

Marsha Sinetar, *Ordinary People as Monks and Mystics*

The peak experience means that a person experiences himself *being* rather than becoming. He also experiences directly—and this is such a difficult point to convey—the Transcendent nature of reality. He enters into the Absolute, becoming one with It, if only for an instant. It is a life-altering instant which many have described as one in which the mind "stops," as a time in which the paradoxical change/changeless nature of the universe opens up.

Or

The peak moment is a time when we come "out" of ourselves and connect with something infinite. This is the moment of full, pure awareness, when the individual feels himself to be the cause of his creations *and* at the same time a part of some expansive, sacred All. This is the time of non-duality. During this moment, the person is most innocent, childlike, spontaneous, vulnerable, unguarded and open. He is all these things because his separateness has ended; he is bonded to a unitive force. This bonding creates—in consciousness and in the physical body as well—feelings of worthiness, compassion, love, of being responsible, capable and fully able to do.

Marilyn Mandala Schlitz, Cassandra Vieten, and Tina Amorok, *Living Deeply*

[*Apollo 14* astronaut **Edgar Mitchell** describes this transformative experience.]

And then, on the way home from the moon, looking out at the heavens, this insight—which I could now call a transcendent experience—happened.

I realized that the molecules of my body had been created or prototyped in an ancient generation of stars—along with the molecules of the spacecraft and my partners and everything else we could see including the Earth out in front of us. Suddenly, it was all very personal. Those were my molecules.

It was an experience of connectedness. It was an experience of bliss, of ecstasy. The type of experience that brings tears to your eyes, you don't know why. Tears of joy, not sadness. This experience continued for three days. I was working. I mean, I had duties to do, but when I was finished with them I would look out the window again and it would start all over. It was so profound. I realized that the story of ourselves as told by science—our cosmology, our religion—was incomplete and likely flawed. I recognized that the Newtonian idea of separate, independent, and discrete things in the universe wasn't a fully accurate description.

And

Native American Lakota elder Gilbert Walking Bull
True spiritual power exists in this world. In our Lakota world, we call it "taku skan skan"—something that moves. What this refers to is how the energy of the Great Spirit, Wakan Tanka Tunkasila, is connected. The atom world is connected to everything Grandfather created. We call it "the Fire Within All Things Moving Alive"—the atom world is this. True spirit is the atom. It is everything. When you know how everything is connected to everything—I grew up knowing this—out of this comes the seven sacred principles connected to our tradition.

Martin Luther King Jr., "Letter from Birmingham Jail"
In a real sense all life is inter-related. All men are caught in an inescapable network of mutuality, tied in a single garment of destiny. Whatever affects one directly, affects all indirectly. I can never be what I ought to be until you are what you ought to be, and you can never be what you ought to be until I am what I ought to be . . .
This is the inter-related structure of reality.

Swami Vivekananda, *Living at the Source,*
Yoga Teachings of Vivekananda
The unity of all existence—you all have it already within yourselves. None was ever born without it. However you may deny it, it continually asserts itself. What is human love? It is more of less the affirmation of that unity: "I am one with thee, my wife, my child, my friend!"
[Also attributed to Vivekananda]
All differences in this world are of degree, and not of kind, because Oneness is the secret of everything.

John Greer, *Seeing, Knowing, Being*

I was sitting in my backyard on a pleasant fall afternoon. I had been reading, but had put my book aside and was just resting in the peaceful beauty of that moment. There was a gentle breeze and leaves were beginning to fall. Without any expectation, in a single instant, outside of time, I realized that life was a seamless unity. It came out of silence with no apparent cause. Sitting there in my neighborhood populated with all the myriad things found in such a setting, from trees, birds, and squirrels to passing cars, the mailman, and the children next door, I knew intuitively that there was no division, no boundaries, no separation—only wholeness. It was an intuitive, gut-level certainty I did not doubt then and have never doubted since. It wasn't an idea or an object that I perceived, *it was what I was*. Afterwards, I sat in stunned silence, with feelings of deep reverence, peace, and humility.

Martha Orton, *Oneness*

If we can grasp, even initially at the intellectual level, the reality of Oneness and the true meaning of this reality, we can come to understand that unity is inherent in all manifestation—earth, mankind, universe, all of it—and that this unity is the fabric of all that is real to us, including the vast variety and range of individuality of humankind. There is Oneness within, which emerges in a multitude of forms and expressions, which is not threatened or changed by individual existence, expression and variety, and does not require absorption or annihilation of the individual's distinctness. This Oneness can be lived, experienced fully, delighted in, while one continues to be oneself. It is the change in perspective, the realization of Oneness which can enable this.

Chapter 5—Oneness as Understood by Others

Eckhart Tolle, *The Power of Now*

Enlightenment . . . is simply your natural state of *felt* oneness with Being. It is a state of connectedness with something immeasurable and indestructible, something that, almost paradoxically, is essentially you and yet is much greater than you. It is finding your true nature beyond name and form. The inability to feel this connectedness gives rise to the illusion of separation, from yourself and from the world around you. You then perceive yourself, consciously and unconsciously, as an isolated fragment. Fear arises, and conflict within and without becomes the norm.

Leo Tolstoy, *War and Peace*

Love is life. All, everything that I understand, I understand only because I love. Everything is, everything exists, only because I love. Everything is united by it alone. Love is God, and to die means that I, a particle of love, shall return to the general and eternal source.

Pierre Teilhard de Chardin, *The Phenomenon of Man*

Love alone is capable of uniting living beings in such a way as to complete and fulfill them, for it alone takes them and joins them by what is deepest in themselves. All we need is to imagine our ability to love developing until it embraces [all living beings] and the earth.

Brian Swimme and Thomas Berry, *The Universe Story*

All that exists in the universe traces back to this exotic, ungraspable seed event, a microcosmic grain, a reality layered with the power to fling a hundred billion galaxies through vast chasms in a flight that has lasted fifteen billion years. The nature of the universe today and of every being in existence is integrally related to the nature of this primordial Flaring Forth. The universe is a single multiform development in which each event is woven together with all others in the fabric of the space-time continuum.

Jiddu Krishnamurti, *The Flame of Attention*

There is no actual duality when you reach a certain state of consciousness—there is only "what is." Duality only exists when you try to deny, or to escape from, "what is" into "what is not."

A famous quote attributed to the Indian mystic and poet—Kabir

All know that the drop merges into the ocean, but few know that the ocean merges into the drop.

There are so many other passages and authors that I wanted to include here—too many to name. But it is good to know that the wisdom of Oneness runs deep and wide in our history, in our present, and hopefully it will become an even greater part of our future. The upcoming and final section of the book is a picture of how I have learned to make these possibilities and this wisdom of Oneness a more practical, and foundational part of my life.

Chapter 6
Thirteen Circles of Timeless Wisdom

Waking Up and Growing Up

Part of my original intention for writing *The Possibilities of Oneness* was to create a simple, clear, and reliable means of continuing to guide myself deeper into those possibilities and into a higher, more inclusive self-knowledge and understanding. As a result of that desire, I realized that I needed to formulate some kind of framework for organizing into a coherent whole all the accumulated yet seemingly disparate insights, life experiences, and wisdom of oneness I had lived and learned up to that point.

By finally writing it down, I was able to do that; I began creating a new and expanded map for myself, one that would be an open and adaptable guide. It would be a way I hoped to provide a constant and inspiring reminder, one not tied to or restricted by any specific religious dogma or rigid belief system, which would encourage and strengthen my ability and resolve to move more consistently toward growth and self-realization. I longed to live in a more meaningful, authentic, and powerful way, with more integrity—and to finally share that wisdom with others.

This eventually led me to create what I refer to as the *thirteen circles of timeless wisdom*, which is a synergistic and inter-supportive circular web of thirteen points of unifying universal human wisdom—open to all. The foundation and structure created by this circle of universal wisdom provides me with a consistent way to move toward a more optimal and integrative way of being and living. One of the most persistent challenges in my growth process has been attempting to bridge the sometimes enormous chasm between an intellectual understanding of Life's wisdom versus the actual lived realization of that wisdom, between the ideal and real action. The wise guidance of the circles of wisdom helps me to cross that gap.

Like most people, I have struggled repeatedly with the limitations and self-imposed suffering that inevitably result from being unable to see the bigger picture and to grow beyond the inherent limitations of an ego-based, separative consciousness. The way we have been taught to relate to the world as separate and isolated selves can become, if we are not intentionally conscious of it, a hopelessly looping madness—a seemingly never-ending vicious circle. That is the incredible power of our human capacity to be self-reflective, to have memory and to form a self-identity.

But it is a power that can go either way: encouraging growth and a healthy understanding and use of our egos, or a mindless and frequently growth-stifling self-centered importance that keeps us locked in the same repeating, draining thoughts and behavioral patterns. And this often happens without us even being aware of the chains we have created for ourselves. The classic Bill Murray movie *Groundhog Day* portrays this lunacy perfectly—the same day lived over and over again with no hope of escape, not even death.

It was this endlessly frustrating cycle of suffering, the sometimes dramatic ups and downs of day-to-day life, that ultimately motivated me to take the next much needed and desired step in my life growth. Sometimes it is just a matter of getting so fed up with the same old story; being stuck in the same broken-record drama to finally motivate real change. That is what finally led me to organize these facets of universal human wisdom into an easily accessible and usable form. These thirteen circles of timeless wisdom provide a deeply rooted base and a way for me to "grow up" and "wake up" at the same time.

Similar to how the contemporary philosopher and significant contributor to an integrative vision Ken Wilber sees it, "waking up" is what I am referring to when I use the expressions "unity experiences," "experiences of Oneness," "flow, wonder, and high peak states," "mystical" or "nondual" experiences—the diverse terms used to refer to those nonthought-based states of consciousness that lie at the heart of experiences of Oneness.

"Growing up," on the other hand, is the natural, normal, and hopefully healthy progression of human growth and development as a whole: becoming the best humans we can be—body, mind, heart, and spirit. In other words, to grow up is to strive to evolve and develop in one's totality—energetically, physically, emotionally, mentally, and spiritually (those intangible higher human potentials) and to realize that growth not only individually, but collectively and ecologically.

To "wake up" is to uncover the transformative power and effect unity experiences can have on us in terms of opening our eyes to the bigger picture of Oneness. It is then taking those life-opening realizations, integrating them, and using them to gradually move into more and more inclusive spheres of awareness and unifying states of consciousness, which then encourages and fortifies our life's unique path of growth and evolution.

Although growing up and waking up may develop independently, they also go hand in hand, serving to support and strengthen the natural unfolding and development of each other. They continually inform each other, ultimately creating a dynamic and building synergy.

It was important to me to portray the wisdom circles clearly, concisely, and simply, avoiding too much explanation in order to leave each point open and adaptable to each person's interpretation, and malleable enough to fit each person's unique life circumstances. The way one uses or understands this wisdom of Oneness is not fixed or inflexible. There is room for adding or subtracting what works best for the individual with respect to fostering and cultivating this integrative wisdom and self-knowledge within each person's unique culture and belief system. To me, the combined path of growing up and waking up epitomizes the ancient and well-known Greek wisdom to "know thyself" in the fullest, most holistic way possible.

Finally, the human wisdom shared in these circles of timeless wisdom belongs to all of us; it has emerged and grown out of thousands of years of human joy and suffering, exploration, learning, and growth, out of the universe's never-ending cycles of life and death, change and transformation. I am a firm believer in our ability to access intuitively and instinctively, if we truly listen, the invaluable, higher wisdom that lies at the heart of our nonrational intellect. It is there that the doorway to the conscious and subconscious possibilities of the human spirit is discovered and opened

Each one of these circles of wisdom could have entire books written about them. I hope only to present what is essential and minimally necessary for "pointing" in the right direction.

Thirteen Circles of Timeless Wisdom

The Center and First Circle
The Source: Life as Infinite, Endless Possibility

This center point and heart of the circles of wisdom is symbolic of our indissoluble unity with the Source of existence itself. It is the expression of the ever-present longing in all of us to somehow know and feel with every vibratory fiber of our being, without doubt or fear, a sense of belonging to the larger cosmic picture of Life in its larger and limitless sense. Expressed in this wisdom is our deep-seated desire to know in our own centers that inconceivable Mystery that is the pulsing living heart of possibility and reality, of all that is, all that might be, all that has passed, and all the possibilities in between.

In this same light, the center point is a mirror of that strongest of our needs to discover a meaningful connection to that which is greater than our individual lives and beyond the bounded sense of self we've created and have become chained to in certain ways. Built into the very fabric of who we are is this calling to seek and to know that which is transcendent and beyond the reach of our senses and the rational mind. And what might be revealed in our search to quench that unshakable desire is that the truth was right there all along.

The wisdom of the first and center circle is the possibility of choosing to become grounded and rooted in this bigger picture of Oneness in a form that best aligns with our loves and dreams and is in harmony with the particulars of our lives as well as the larger whole. This is the wisdom that continually reminds us to open and anchor our conscious awareness, our entire being—body, mind, heart, and spirit—to a more expansive, unifying, and meaningful paradigm rather than to the extremely limiting and disjointed one that we have become largely stuck in and blinded by.

Every chapter of this book is my version of that vision; for others the possibilities are open and many. This wellspring of wisdom, however it takes shape, then becomes our fundamental impetus and guiding power, enabling us to gradually move and transform consciousness into its expanded and integrative possibilities.

A crucially important point to be mindful of here is that it makes no difference if a person (or group of people) is religious or an atheist, spiritual or agnostic, scientifically inclined or not, a materialist or an idealist, a believer or nonbeliever—or some combination of all of the above. Despite what and how we believe individually and collectively, the answers to the larger questions in life are not written in stone and do not belong to any one person or particular group of people. Hopefully we have the freedom to decide how we see and act in relation to Life's larger questions. The answers to those questions will change and grow as we do.

It is our intrinsic power to choose how we believe, feel, and direct our energy, vision, and purpose in terms of shaping our own lives and the lives of others for the greater good. With that power though, we must also remember to steer clear of mistaking the symbols, images, words, and all the many ways used to "point" to Ultimate Reality, however conceived, as more real, true, or important than the Source from which those maps and constructs arise in the first place. The qualities and descriptions we attempt to project onto our ideas of Life, God, Spirit, and all the rest of the words we use to point to Infinity are always only human concepts, relative and conditional, and therefore limited in terms of their absolute truth. To make the mistake of identifying with and defending these concepts as ultimate is to tread on potentially dangerous ground. It sometimes turns into one group's beliefs being viewed as the only right way or superior to another's, then used as justification for hatred and violence toward those who don't see the world in the same way.

Without the wisdom of discovering and creating a rootedness and continuous connection to the Spirit and Oneness of Life, we too easily lose contact with a bigger, kinder, and more inclusive picture of things; cut off from our Source, we become lost in the clouding veil of separation and aloneness. The center of the circle becomes our center for creating and sustaining a foundation in and connection to the greater whole, as a continually available reference point and reminder to envision and strive to grow out of a separative, self-centered, isolated mode of consciousness into an ever-expanding, more inclusive, and unitive one.

The Second Circle
Realizing and Living Life's Many Possibilities

The second circle of timeless wisdom is symbolic of the One blossoming into and becoming the many; it is limitless Being or Life creatively pouring forth and becoming the endless diversity of our universe. Again, like the Ocean and its waves it is a beautiful symphonic movement from possibility to actuality, from pure potential to manifest reality. The second circle is the first point on the bigger circle arising directly from the center and source nexus. It represents the wisdom of creating a unifying and growth-guiding vision and life path that emerges out of and in harmony with the vast genius and creativity of the universal story itself, in which we and everything else are inextricably linked and reflected.

While the first and center core circle is an awakening awareness of our rootedness in and Oneness with Life, the second wisdom circle is about harmonizing with and optimizing the unique potentialities to be uncovered and realized by each of us within this greater cosmic unfolding. The human drive and motivation to learn, to grow, to feel, and know the world in increasingly deeper and more expansive ways is unquestionable. A truly defining characteristic of being human is our insatiable curiosity; it is our unstoppable desire to know more and to become more.

The larger vision that has emerged for me in relation to the wisdom of this second circle is to consistently and intentionally learn to grow and develop in the most integrative and holistic way possible: with body, mind, heart, and spirit, as an individual and as a whole, continually informed and expanded by experiences of Oneness. It is growing up and waking up in a way that encourages an amplifying synergy between both.

These are only basic and possible ingredients and a starting point for growing into our greater potentials and for waking up to increasing spheres of awareness and Oneness. How they are envisioned, empowered, and acted upon is open to each of us, depending on our chosen paths in life, our circumstances and experience, our knowledge, dreams, and passions. For me the unitive wisdom of the thirteen circles is part of a simple and clear map for realizing the above vision. Life is at its best and most beautiful when the heart of our being is awakened to the Oneness that is its source, and with that wisdom we can learn to love, revel in, and create our best lives within this miraculous multiplicity we call reality.

The Third Circle
Love Is Oneness—the Grand Unifier

Love is notoriously difficult to pin down. It is elusive and defies definition because it is in reality a dynamic, ever-changing profusion of layered feelings, varied degrees of emotion, and a collage of thoughts and images tied to some of our deepest desires. Love is multidimensional and possesses a range of meanings. It can be imagined as white light being focused and directed through a prism: What is revealed is a rainbow of radiant colors and possibilities hidden within what appears to be only whiteness. Volumes have been written about the enormity of love with the hope of getting to its essence, but its mystery often remains. In the end it must be a learned and lived experience.

The third circle of wisdom is about growing into this higher understanding of love. The more profound experiences of Oneness are at their core experiences of the highest form of love: love without conditions, love for its own sake, pure and freely given and openly received. It is not the twists and turns, ups and downs of romantic, idealized, or commercialized love; there are no ifs, ands, or buts about this higher, more inclusive love; it is love no matter what, unbounded by thought or selfish motives and desires. It is this more expansive and inclusive love that is the root of all other types of love.

Love at this level is both an innate knowing (even if not a fully conscious one), as well as the learned ability to see and act on the unifying and underlying Oneness we all share—with one another and life as a whole. It is knowing without reservation that the person we normally perceive as other, as different, as separate, who we "label" in countless ways is in reality the same shared "being" and "presence" that I am. We and the other are one, one and the same essence, one and the same shared ocean of awareness. It is the reason many people will willingly risk their lives to save the life of another—even a stranger.

In this way, love might be viewed as the feeling aspect of Oneness; it is "felt Oneness"—the lived and emotive experience of wholeness and connectedness—love as the grand unifier. It is an ever-present gravitational pull toward Oneness, the spark that can ignite genuine empathy and compassion. It calls throughout existence not only for union, but also for the realization of the true, the good, the beautiful, and for greater awareness. Love is the pull of a higher purpose, away from separation and toward wholeness and union.

Selfish, self-centered desires, if allowed to rule our days, blind and pull us toward contraction; love pulls the other way—toward the realization of compassion and Oneness. The more we are held by the gravitational chains of self-centeredness or allow an ego-centered state to be our primary mode of consciousness, the less likely it will be for genuine love and Oneness to be learned and experienced.

The usual movement and inclination of love, if unimpeded and encouraged to flow and grow naturally, is to gradually expand into greater, more-inclusive circles of awareness and compassion. It is a natural progression from love that is self-centered and selfish, to a "self-love" that is healthy and able to love others as a reflection of learning to love oneself. It will grow from there into a love that knows and feels others as one, expanding outward into a love of and Oneness with the world, with the universe, with God, Spirit, Life, or Source—a complete love and Oneness with all and everything. Each increasing level of love opens to include more in its embrace, larger feelings and acts of compassion, care, and a growing sense of connectedness.

Love is there, like an ever-present river, but we have to intentionally tap its potentials; we have to jump in, taste its waters, get to know its intricacies, subtleties, and depths, its rising and falling currents and flow. And most important, we must be open and vulnerable to the inevitable suffering and pain that will come with the loss of who and what we love. If we can do that, if we can find the courage to face that darkness, it will enlarge our hearts' reach and our ability to love in a higher and larger way. Higher love is the key that opens the door into the possibilities of greater Oneness, meaning, and joy.

Life will teach each of us about love, but we can also strive to create the conditions for love to flourish. And like experiences of Oneness, we will know that love cannot be forced or truly controlled—as much as we'd like to think it can. No matter what life deals us though, we can still stoke the possibilities of love and compassion that have been buried by pain, suffering, and misunderstanding. A higher and unlimited love that arises from the wisdom of Oneness has the power to bring us out of even the darkest and most hateful places. It is the only power that can in the end.

This quote attributed to the mystic poet Rumi says it perfectly.

"Your task is not to seek for love, but merely to seek and find all the barriers within yourself that you have built against it."

The Fourth Circle
Energy Is Everything—Making the Most of It

Energy, as we have come to understand it, is the quintessential basis and source of all that is possible in our universe in relation to change, movement, growth, and the ongoing cycles of life and death. Energy is the fundamental potential and capacity of our universe for creation, manifestation, and destruction. It is the power that is inherent in all that is—animate and inanimate; it is part of what makes our universe dynamic, lively, interconnected, and one.

It was Einstein's quantum leap in understanding about energy that revealed to the world this One energy hidden in all that exists—$E=mc^2$. Energy equals mass (a measure of matter) multiplied by the speed of light squared (a very large number). In plain words, Einstein's famous equation shows that matter is in essence energy, unimaginably huge amounts of potential energy. It is the same energy seen on an infinitesimally small scale in the explosion of an atomic bomb (nuclear fission or fusion) and on an immense scale in the power that ignites and sustains stars such as our sun (nuclear fusion). That same potential energy is the basis and essence of our bodies, of every cell, muscle, and hair, of every thought, feeling, and action.

Energy is the heart of life, and life at its core is an ever-present, ebbing and flowing rhythm of change, flux, and transformation. Energy is that which enables the infinite potential of Life in a big sense to explore and manifest the endless expressions of life in a finite sense. Energy is not so much a thing as it is an empowering process. As science has revealed to us, although energy can be transformed from one of its many forms to another, it cannot be lost. It seems unlimited in its possibilities, yet for biological beings the energy available for daily life is limited, so an informed and intelligent use of that energy is vital.

The fourth circle then is the ever-important reminder to live in a way that most efficiently and sagaciously conserves, uses, and optimizes our life energies on a day-to-day basis. It is learning and becoming acutely aware of the critical connection between energy, health, and wholeness at all levels of our lives. This fourth facet of wisdom is ultimately learning about and living in a way that makes the most of the quality, quantity, and vitality of the energy we acquire through the air we breathe, the water we drink, the food we eat, the way we keep our bodies tuned up, in shape, healthy, and well, the people we choose to have in our lives, and all the countless ways we interact energetically with the world around us. These choices then become the habits that translate directly into the vibrancy, healthiness, and the levels of energy that compose and animate our bodies, minds, hearts, and spirits.

Educating ourselves, paying close attention to and intentionally choosing the healthiest ways of using the many forms of energy that support and nourish our daily lives is essential. Most people will agree and know at some level that good health, as far as is possible for each person, is one of the most necessary and basic ingredients for a fulfilling and happy life. Without it life can be a difficult and dark road. Many of the things we thought mattered most in our lives, that we have spent so much time and energy pursuing, lose importance and appeal rapidly when faced with a debilitating, life-changing illness. One of the marvels of the human body though is that for the most part it is born hardwired for health and built to function naturally at an optimal level—if treated with the wisdom of a healthy energy cultivation and use.

Of equal importance to knowing how energy relates to health, is learning to see the huge amounts of energy needed to placate and sustain a separative, fear-based consciousness. Becoming aware of those points of energy drainage and learning to uproot and transform the conditioning that causes such a tremendous loss of energy is hugely important for our growth into higher levels of consciousness. I am reminded how to do this by the wisdom held in all the other circles of wisdom.

The vital energy that continually and dynamically suffuses and moves in and through us, like the energy that moves through the ocean as waves, is the power needed for the realization and enjoyment of life itself, for fulfilling its deeper meanings and wider possibilities. Energy, healthy energy, which should ideally be equally available to all, is the foundation for human growth, awakening, and transformation. Making the most of that energy then is vital.

The Fifth Circle
Breaking Free of Ego, Seeing the Truth

As certain spiritual traditions and even modern science hold, what we call the "self" or "ego"—those life processes that we identify with as an actual, real, and separately existing entity—is an illusion, a continually perpetuated mirage of the thinking mind. Yet think of all the trouble, pain, and suffering this particular mirage of consciousness can cause if not seen and understood for what it is. Ego, in truth, is a point of reference, a concept and convention that helps to build and maintain a consensual reality. But it is a constructed identity that is empty of any essential or actual reality. It is temporary, ephemeral, and ever-changing, transforming moment to moment like all of life.

In other words, there is nothing fixed or permanent about the self; the self arises out of the flow and unfolding of the universe in the form of human life and awareness. And the universe is a never-ending transformation of energy in motion and flux. To say that there is a self or ego separate from the stream of Life is like collecting a bucket of water from a vast and deeply flowing river and declaring that the water in that bucket is the truth of the running river itself. When we attach to or become overly identified with this fabricated sense of a separate self, we stop the flow of Life. By stopping that natural flow, fear arises—fear that exists only in our minds as thoughts of loss or not having enough.

The fifth circle is the wisdom of breaking through to the truth of what the ego actually is and does and discovering the freedom possible outside of its walls. Put another way, it is finally realizing and waking up to the limits of a mind-generated, thought-sustained belief in a separate self. It is about liberating awareness from its jailor, the gravitational pull and contraction of an ego-dominated, separative consciousness and moving intentionally and fearlessly to embrace the wider spheres of an integrative, unitive consciousness—our amazing human potential. Our egos become the tool for that transformation, instead of the barrier.

And the freedom that I mention here is not the freedom to get or to do or to have whatever is wanted when it is wanted, or to go wherever and whenever one desires; it is instead the real freedom that comes with freeing ourselves from the conditioning that allows a contracted, small-mindedness to run our lives. That kind of freedom is available to all of us, anytime and anyplace. That is true freedom.

So what do we do then, how do we break through to the truth of ego? Consciousness, thought, and other activities of the mind abound in paradox. How is it possible for the ego to get outside of itself or to think it can somehow "get rid" of itself? That is akin to attempting to get unstuck from glue with glue, or using a sword to cut itself in half. The idea of actually being able to permanently delete our sense of self, the ego—our navigation and operating system—from our lives is a contradiction and would lead to massive chaos if it were actually possible. It would be like everyone deciding to fly in planes that had no pilots, no directional systems, and no organized communications or safety systems—but are still able to get off the ground.

If we had no sense of self we would have no way to relate with one another, to communicate and to progress intelligently as a species. The ego is only a problem when it is not understood for what it is—an amalgam of energetic, physical, mental, emotional, and spiritual processes that are pathways for Life. The problematic and challenging part is when we are so identified with those processes that we become truly blinded and indifferent to the bigger picture. The wave becomes so clouded, so ensnared in its own reflections that it sees nothing else. The Ocean and its source of greater possibilities are obscured and lost to it. There is no higher connection and very little meaning other than satisfying selfish desires. That is what I mean by small-mindedness.

Instead of having an egocentric, separative consciousness as our primary awareness and operating mode, by seeing the truth of ego we can begin to transform that foundational awareness toward a unitive consciousness. Ironically we need our egos to do that, but only up to a point. Then ego must be disengaged and set aside until needed. In other words, we learn to control those ego-based, life-shaping processes; they no longer control us. How do we do this? Presence (the upcoming circle) is the key to seeing through the folly of allowing our egos and self-importance to run our lives. And unity experiences are our wake-up calls to return to presence and for realizing that underlying truth of Oneness and love that are often obscured by the ego's fears and demands.

It is critical that we begin to recognize as individuals and as a world collective that consciousness driven by ego-generated selfishness and self-centeredness must be outgrown and shifted to a nondominant, more subservient place in our lives. The potential consequences of not doing so will simply keep us stuck in the same historical patterns of divisiveness, fear, greed, violence, and self-interest that we are entrenched in today—the reason history tends to repeat itself. It's as if humanity overall developed to the teenage stage and then stopped. This is not to say that we haven't done some amazing things as a species. We are intelligent beings after all, but intelligence without an equal growth in awareness can be a potentially dangerous and consciousness-stifling imbalance.

The Sixth Circle
Returning to the Power of Presence—Clearing the Way

The sixth circle is remembering to live from the deep well of wisdom called "presence." Presence is human awareness centered and rooted in the timeless, dimensionless, ever-present Now. It is the pure awareness that is often referred to as our "true, unveiled, and unclouded natures." Through presence we see and know the true limitations of our egos directly, without thought or judgment.

But true presence is a rare experience in modern times. So often it is clouded by the same thought- and self-dominated consciousness described in the previous circle. Presence is often covered over by the haze of the mind's continual activity, and it is only regained through stillness and by reembodying the gap, the spaciousness between our thoughts. Presence is the transparent, radiant waters of Being and Awareness before being clouded by self-absorption, by the fears and worries of past and future. In presence we return to the awareness that is the foundation of existence, as it is empty and clear of the forms of reality that define it, organize it, and give it shape.

And contrary to how we may often feel, presence is our deepest being and impossible to lose; it is the ever-abiding heart of who we are. Presence is like the sun in that way, continually present despite our feeling like it has disappeared, covered over by passing clouds or veiled by the spinning planet itself. In our busyness to get somewhere and be someone, we lose touch with the power of presence in which we are rooted. The wave forgets that it is one with the Ocean. How then do we remember; how do we wake up to the greater truth of Oneness and presence that is always with us? The most direct and well-known path for clearing those clouds, waking up, and for making presence a more constant part of our lives is through a simple meditative practice.

By meditation I'm referring to some consistent practice that helps us return to a more subjectively objective perspective where it becomes possible to step back, to witness and observe consciousness, to "watch" and "disengage" from thoughts instead of being caught up by and identified with them. Through meditation we eventually learn to stop mistaking the thoughts that "we have" for who we really are in our depths: pure, spacious, open awareness.

Some form of meditation is the way through these obscuring and mesmerizing mists of the conditioned mind. I like to call it "clearing the way." Regular meditation or clearing the way becomes our tool for transforming consciousness from a separative, divisive awareness into a unitive awareness, from small mind to big, open mind, from a contracted life to an expansive life. It is the invaluable key that helps us to unlock and recover what is in reality our ever-present, natural, spontaneous, and optimal way of being and doing.

Attention directed to the movement and feeling of breathing is, I believe, the most natural, accessible, and simplest way to meditate. Breath is life; it is always close at hand, right there and easy to tune into, and awareness easily follows and is opened up by our breath. By focusing on the movement of our breathing, awareness through attention is allowed to move out of the head, away from thinking, into the heart, the abdomen, the limbs, and into the entire body. It will actually begin to feel like every cell in the body is breathing. In this way, mind activity is stilled, we get outside of our thoughts, and awareness is finally allowed to open up and become "embodied" presence. This shift in conscious awareness can change everything because it is the beginning of finally knowing and feeling presence again. With each new breath the energy of life enlivens this feeling.

A variety of great books is out there on the many proven benefits of meditation and mindfulness, along with the different ways to meditate, so I won't go into any more detail about specific techniques. In general and after many years of meditating, the single-most important realization to me has been: Keep it as simple as possible. The less that there is "in mind" and the fewer tricks and preconceptions to start with, the better. Simplicity and clarity are essential because the true purpose of meditation is to drop all devices, "all practices," and enter into a space of presence without method, without controlling effort. Meditation is aimed at surrendering with trust, acceptance, nonattachment, and with love to what is, and to regain our natural state of presence. It is about finally dropping any and all technique and realizing that presence, the stillness and peace of being, has never left us.

Meditation is also learning to disengage the thinking mind by directing our attention to focus on something or some activity other that thought. That way the possibilities of awareness—that have been limited and contracted for so long by a misplaced belief in a self that is thought to exist in our heads and behind our eyes—can begin to expand into the heart, the body, and beyond. With time and persistence, meditation helps us to loosen our self-created boundaries, to stretch them so that they become more encompassing and inclusive. Our ability to empathize, to see ourselves as a part of and one with the world around us begins to grow; genuine compassion begins to emerge.

The ego is about self-centeredness and control. Meditation is our way of seeing through those limitations by learning to be still, to let go, let be, and let happen; it is cultivating the ability to drop the need to control, manipulate, and have the world always be exactly the way we think it should be. It is the best and most effective way to learn how to witness thoughts instead of being trapped by them. Some form of presence practice ultimately becomes that effortless effort that can open us to the pure and fundamental awareness and boundlessness, the living presence and unifying power underneath all the many coverings of self and personality. Meditation is simultaneously a pathway back to presence and presence itself. And unity experiences are glimpses of the possibilities of that presence.

Being the lover of water that I am, a helpful analogy for visualizing the meditative process is to imagine trying to stay afloat at the surface of a turbulent, frothy, whirling, and swirling whitewater-covered ocean. The turbulence at the surface of this ocean symbolizes the mind's endless activity: our sense of self—thoughts, emotions, feelings, desires, wants, likes, and dislikes. It is ego as doer, planner, defender, seeker, and controller and all its many other roles. Attempting to paddle and swim gets extremely tiring and stressful in these conditions. Meditation is a way of steadily releasing, relaxing, and relinquishing that limiting and draining need to always be in control of life, often those parts of life that are beyond our control anyway. Through meditation we learn to fully surrender to the powerful stillness that lies just under the mind's turbulent surface, in the ineffable depths of our being. We grow to trust those depths, to let go and fall back into the power of presence, into a wide-open spaciousness empty of effort, form, or thought.

Thoughts come and go, rise and fall, take form and disappear. Our unique human capacity and power to be self-aware, to be aware that we are aware, is what enables us to watch this thought stream and pull ourselves out of it. We learn to disengage, detach, and observe silently, seeing finally that although thoughts have tremendous creative power and potential, they are only energy that is momentarily given a particular form. And although they may arise repeatedly, out of habit, they are transient and ephemeral. They are not who and what we are in truth.

That is a monumental realization when it happens. We can and do continually shape reality, both consciously and unconsciously, with our thoughts, along with all the feelings, desires, attitudes, and beliefs those thoughts help to create and sustain. But to reemphasize, we only "have thoughts"; we are not those thoughts in heart and essence. We all know how habitual patterns of thinking can take us places we don't want to go, to feel things we don't want to feel. Meditation helps us detach from identifying with our incessant self-talk and constant commentary so that we are not so beguiled and entranced by it. We learn to rein in and to direct thoughts more intentionally, with clearer vision in a more conscious and powerful way—aligned with a higher source of wisdom. Because our thoughts have the power to shape our reality, we must make sure that we direct that power consciously with vision and intention, instead of allowing conditioned habits of thinking to run our lives like mindless robots.

The wisdom of the sixth circle is learning to regain presence in our lives through a persistent meditative practice. Living with increasing presence is one of the most significant actions we can do as humans to encourage and accelerate growth and realization. And it is never too late to start; countless scientific studies and thousands of years of human experience have demonstrated repeatedly the unquestionable transformative power of meditation, of nowfulness, awarefulness, and presence in our lives. It is a readily accessible and practical means for unlocking the amazing potentials of consciousness open to all of us.

The Seventh Circle
A Clear Vision of Our Creative Potentials

The seventh circle is the wisdom of recognizing and realizing our inherent creative powers, those creative capacities that we all share and that are a mirror of the universal creative dynamic itself. In our depths we have an irrefutable desire to create, and we usually feel at our best when we are immersed in the creative act. In fact, it is often during moments of intense, absorbing creativity when profound feelings of presence and Oneness can begin to be felt.

But to our disadvantage, we often take for granted this seemingly common-sense ability to act in the world, to create, and to choose how we live our lives. In light of that tendency, it is important to look at the true power and potential of the creative process in more detail. That way we will more likely be inclined to make it an intentional part of our lives—instead of just a random, directionless habit. When the creative dynamic is harnessed to its fullest, we are enabled to realize our life's highest visions in the best and most effective way possible.

Here is a distilled snapshot of how I have come to understand the creative pathway. It is one very simple way of seeing this ever-important creative dynamic, but certainly not the only.

To begin with is the *Will of Life* itself: The universal principle that permeates and moves all of existence toward increasing levels of complexity and novelty, despite the opposing effects of chaos and entropy. It is the creative power latent in our cosmos to move, explore, and direct the possibilities of energy into continually changing and newer forms. This larger *Will of Life* is reflected in microcosmic form as *human will*, which is then informed and channeled through the organizing infrastructure of the mind as ego (self and personality). In this way, human will is purposefully changed into a clear and meaningful *intention* that then directs awareness in the form of focused *attention* into *action* (or nonaction)—unfolding as the *creative act*.

This is a powerful formula for realizing our dreams and visions. But how do we make the most of this creative dynamic? The essential first step is to learn how each aspect of the formula fits and works together.

All life has at its core the *"will"* not only to be and to exist, but also to "become," to act, to do, to seek and explore, to continue its own existence, and to move from pure possibility to that which is actual and real. For humans it is not only the "will to survive" but also the will to learn, grow, and become more. Will is the foundational volition of life; as a mirror of its universal form, will is the human power to channel, direct, move, and shape energy—to change, transform, create, or destroy.

Will itself is not a thought, a feeling, a desire, or a means of control; it is fundamental and prior to those human capacities. It can be informed by them, but it is not defined by them. Human will is visceral and deep. It can be strengthened or used at a higher level of functioning, in harmony with the universal order and rhythm. It can be drawn upon to shift into a unitive and integrative consciousness or it can be left to the dictates and confining limitations of a separative consciousness. That becomes our choice.

Intention is what will transforms into once it is within the organizing framework and vision-creating powers of the ego. Each person's will is informed and sculpted by that individual's unique mix of desire, feeling, energy, intuition, intelligence, creativity, and imagination and in this way will becomes an *intention*. Otherwise, willpower is like an arrow unleashed without a target. To "set an intention" means the will has been given a clear and defined target, a target that has been vividly imagined with all the senses, a lucid vision energized by the shaping forces of emotion, thought, and belief.

Attention is essentially focused awareness. It is the spotlight of consciousness and our way of relating to the world in an organized and orderly fashion—as a self. By way of the focusing power of awareness, each of us is able to selectively and attentively be aware of what might otherwise be an overwhelming barrage of sensory data, thoughts, feelings, and everything else in the world. In other words, to direct attention is our ability to focus awareness on the world as the specific contents of consciousness at that moment.

Attention is one of our most valuable and potent human assets because it is through attention, guided by clear intentions, that we act and create. But attention is a power that is rarely used to its fullest potential. It can be scattered, unfocused, and distracted or it can be concentrated and powerful like a razor-sharp laser. Attention can also be both focused and expansive at the same time, which is exactly what certain unity experiences feel like.

With the above capacity to creatively guide our lives, we all have the potential to participate more intentionally in the creation of our individual and collective reality, utilizing our egos in a more conscious way. It is our means of discovering and empowering life's higher visions and dreams. If we listen closely, with a balance of body, mind, heart, and spirit, and if we pay attention to the subtle hints, signs, and indications guiding us to align with our highest path in life, making the right choices at the right time and place will start becoming more common and clearer. Life begins falling into accord with our profoundest and truest desires, and we fall into harmony and love with life.

Finally, and this is key, the highest expression of this creative dynamic is discovered when we learn to embrace and vividly imagine our intentions and our visions with the highest good in mind and then release them—letting go of the need to control any specific outcome. With complete trust, surrender, without attachment, and with the truest gratitude, we send those clearly intended visions into the heart of the universe and into our deepest being, knowing that they are one, and that those envisioned dreams are already a reality.

With patience, those visions will then be reflected back to us in the form of the intuitions and the opportunities we need to guide us and make them a reality. Again, this is an enormously powerful force in our lives to purposefully create a life and a path with compassion and in the spirit of the greater good, truth, and beauty of the world.

The best things that have happened to me took place when I was willing and able to let go completely, to trust and detach from any expected outcome, and to be fully open and welcoming to whatever unfolded. What Life manifests in return may not always be exactly what we "thought" we wanted, but it is often even better, especially when finally seen from within the larger perspective of experience and hindsight.

The Eighth Circle
Keeping the Course—Authenticity and Integrity

The wisdom of the eighth circle is guiding oneself to stay on course and true to the "right and higher path." It is a conscious map for navigating the precarious and often relative terrain of truth. Truth, the way that I mean it here, is the common and agreed upon sense of what is considered good and right—or not, and all the layers in between. It is to know in our hearts what we should or ought to do and making the wisest choices in any given situation for the greatest good, not only from a personal viewpoint but from a collective and universal one. It is the proverbial moral compass guiding one to live a life of both integrity and authenticity.

According to Merriam-Webster's online dictionary, "integrity" has two definitions: It means being honest and having strong moral principles, as well as being whole and undivided. "Authenticity," in a similar way and in its simplest form, means being genuine, real, and true. Given those meanings, it is easy to see how these two words would complement each other.

To me, to live authentically and with integrity means that a person's thoughts, words, feelings, beliefs, attitudes, values, and actions are true to, and, as much as possible, in harmony with and genuinely reflective of a higher guiding vision. And by "higher vision" I am referring to a more encompassing vision originating out of a growing understanding of love, Oneness, and compassionate action. Then actions align and are true to wisely informed and independently derived beliefs—beliefs that emerge out of a growing awareness of our unified relationship with others, with life, and the world as a whole.

In this way too, words and deeds become genuine and consistent reflections of our highest values—values that have emerged from the life experience and intelligence acquired through presence and a continual questioning and reflecting of what matters most in life. The need for artificiality and pretense is burned away in the light of these powerful human potentials. What is right, what is good, true, ethical, and in accord with the larger universal harmony unfolds naturally, unimpeded by conditioned thinking and freed from mindless actions.

I think most of us feel that at some point in life we just know without having to think too much about it what is right or wrong, good, truthful, and beneficial—not only to oneself but to the whole. A potential issue with that belief though, and a reason to have a moral compass always on hand nevertheless, is that our capacity to rationalize, to justify, defend, and push on others what "we think, know, and feel" to be right can be completely mistaken, misleading, and delusional.

If in doubt, one might ask (as a kind of synthesis of the Golden Rule and Kant's moral philosophy): Does the choice being considered, if acted upon, lead to greater harmony, balance, and love in the world at all levels and would it create greater overall health and well-being, wholeness, and integrity at an individual level, as a species, and in relation to life as a whole? It is a big question, but one that we can intuit in our minds and hearts.

Hitler would be one of the darkest examples of what a severely twisted and delusional rationalization can lead to in the most extreme of cases; he not only ignorantly convinced himself that the horrific torture and death of thousands of innocent human beings was right and justifiable, but he also managed to create an environment that manipulated thousands of others to believe in and act on his same sick and warped ideas. That is consciousness at its pathological worst.

The Ninth Circle
Three Keys as One—Trust, Acceptance, and Nonattachment

The ninth circle of timeless wisdom is a reminder to stay close to and to continually move toward the realization of three life-changing ways of seeing, relating, and acting in the world: trust, acceptance, and nonattachment. These are the three keys that are one. They are each slightly different actions and ways of approaching life, from subtly different angles, but with the same overall intention and desire behind them: to help move beyond the limits of a self-centered consciousness and the constant need to control what are often uncontrollable aspects of life.

These three keys are an intuitive as well as learned ability to purposefully and consciously free ourselves from the stress, limitations, and draining effects of always feeling the need to control life. Control manifests in many ways, ways that are not always immediately obvious. It is often a two-sided effort. On one side there is the drive to avoid, resist, run away from, and deny what we dislike or what doesn't fit our particular version and expectations for reality; while on the other side there is a forcing of a selfishly guided will, manipulation, a pushing and pulling, a chasing after, seeking and striving for what we do want and like, a race to possess and become the things that do fit our model of how we think the world should or shouldn't be.

Trust, acceptance, and nonattachment are parts of the human potential for moving beyond a fear-based awareness into a trust-based awareness. Each is an expression of the natural intelligence that arises out of the wisdom of presence. The opposite of living with presence is to live confined by the web of time and in the grip of ego. In this state, consciousness often manifests as distrust, resistance, fighting life and what is, demanding and expecting life to be a certain way, blaming, complaining, and projecting. Eventually awareness begins to contract and can with time start to close off; our minds become increasingly narrowed by thoughts that continually generate looping fears and negative emotions.

Trust in its larger sense is a deep and certain knowing, the felt intuition that whatever is arising right now, good or bad, is what it is, as it is, and nothing else—regardless of what we expect, demand, or are told it should be. Trust is the opposite of fear; it is fear's resolution. It is learning to be okay with the circumstances of life no matter what, where, when, why, or how they are at that time, from a place of balanced composure and equanimity. It is also knowing and trusting that life, in whatever way it is expressing itself in that particular moment, will with certainty invariably change, as it always does.

Likewise, *trust* is a deep-seated confidence that despite the chance and randomness of our universe, there are also threads of unifying meaning woven within that uncertainty. Experiences of Oneness strengthen a trusting relationship to life because the profounder meaning that permeates existence is experienced and known directly through those experiences. The little things, the pettiness that might have bothered us before begins to diminish in the light of those realizations.

Acceptance is the twin of trust. It is the choice and attitude that enables trust to happen in the first place. It is first the decision to begin releasing and relinquishing the ego-generated resistance and the drive to control what is often beyond control. Acceptance is our empowering capacity to say a full-hearted and genuine "yes" to who we are and what is happening in any given moment without judgment, fear, or the need for whatever is unfolding to be other that what it is—to be different or better, less or more, to stop or to continue. Acceptance in this light is first a full and compassionate acceptance of oneself and then the ability to extend that same feeling and respect to others.

Trust and acceptance are inseparable. And acceptance does not mean giving in or giving up in some fatalistic, apathetic, doom-and-gloom way. Instead, it is learning to accept what is at the same time that one is motivated and inspired to change for the better what is possible to change, like the words of wisdom expressed in the Serenity Prayer: "Grant me the serenity to accept the things I cannot change, courage to change the things I can, and wisdom to know the difference."

Nonattachment also fits perfectly with acceptance and trust. It is the gradual and liberating ability to free oneself from holding too tightly and being tied to any particular outcome in relation to all our many dreams and desires. It is the learned ability to let go of the thoughts, the idealized expectations, and controlling demands on life that it be or happen in a preconceived way, other than what is in the moment—perfectly imperfect. Attachment to anything is in essence a need to control it, the fear of losing it, or the unrealistic demand that it be what we think it should be rather than what it is.

Nonattachment is instead an attitude of freedom; it is when self-centered expectations, which are frequently the triggers of negative emotions if not met, are turned instead into *"preferences."* A preference is much different from an expectation. A preference is to "prefer" that life be a certain way but no longer in an emotionally attached way—or at least we are much less attached. This is an optimal way of being and acting in the world, freeing us and saving titanic amounts of energy.

Letting go, letting be, and letting happen really sums it all up: To let go of and "surrender" the incessant ego-centered drive to control is to align, tune, and flow with the deeper currents of Life as Infinite. It is also learning to accept and trust the natural rhythms and patterns of life as finite, the particular and the universal. By saying that, I am not insinuating that we trust everything in some sort of childlike and naïve way. It is rather a suggestion that we trust Life from the larger understanding and intelligence of Oneness. Instead of resistance, instead of self-centeredness, we simply become centered. We return to the present moment, to nowfulness as it is in all of its marvelous expressiveness. To let be and let happen is to speak and act in the spirit of a full-hearted and affirmative "yes" to life as it is—without regret, selfishness, or reservation.

The Tenth Circle
Growing Gratitude

The timeless wisdom of the tenth circle is the wise reminder to continually open to and grow into ever-broadening and more-inclusive spheres of gratitude. Gratitude is the genuinely heartfelt recognition and acknowledgment of the people, events, things, places—all the many aspects and happenings of life that add a true measure of joy to our days, that impact us in meaningful and enriching ways. It may be something significant or subtle, positive or even negative. A sense of gratitude can be a perfect jumping-off point for getting outside of a self-absorbed and egotistical mindset. It opens awareness to include a wider and kinder vision of the world.

Gratitude, appreciation, thankfulness and reverence are all clear pathways to love and Oneness, connectedness and belonging. While love is the mighty trunk and the mother of all we call good, beautiful, and fulfilling in life, gratitude is one of its deepest roots. Experiencing genuine gratitude can be the one feeling that makes a day worthwhile, adding meaning and value to that day. To the extent that we are able to generate and share feelings of thankfulness is the degree to which we are also able to move toward a feeling of "love." Energized and intentional gratitude can be a deeply satisfying, simple, and always obtainable way of feeling Oneness with the world around us and for moving from a separative consciousness to a unifying one.

The beginning point for me is gratitude for Life in its big sense, for the utter miracle and wonder of existence itself. This reverential sense of appreciation is closely in tune with trust; it is simultaneously being able to trust and be grateful for our individual lives as they are right here and right now, as they only can be, unfolding in harmony with the larger universal rhythms of which we are each individually and collectively an expression.

The greatest challenge for me has been and continues to be finding gratitude even when life isn't going as planned, even if it is the exact opposite of what I want or expect it to be. That is big gratitude. In this way, to be grateful is ultimately about discovering and giving thanks from our hearts and deepest being for all the countless factors that add significance and value to our lives, even if that particular day has been a difficult or dark one.

It is important to also point out that authentic gratitude is not an obligation or a forced reciprocation for kind words or deeds. In its truest sense and in its purest form gratitude, like love, is simple, spontaneous, and flows naturally of its own accord by being freely and unconditionally shared and accepted. It is being able to give and receive thanks without attachment or the need to say more—other than "thank you." Attachment, selfish motives, or expectations bind and limit gratitude, change it into a lesser form. In its highest expression, gratitude is discovered in presence and is the powerful recognition and honoring of the Life and Oneness we all share.

During experiences of Oneness there is often an unstoppable bursting forth of heart-opening gratitude. It is a feeling that is intimately intertwined with the lived experiences and feelings of wonder, deep contentment, and mystery. Gratefulness that is brimming with this uncontainable joy is a truly unifying and beautiful experience. It is the kind of joy that is at times filled with both marrow-deep laughter and tears of exultant bliss.

And these words do not even begin to touch those feelings of aliveness and gratitude that can move like waves through heart and spirit during deeper experience of Oneness. The magic is to let the thankfulness pour in and out of our beings, flowing freely, filling and emptying into the world and back again, satisfying the soul's yearning for connection and union. There is no other experience and realization so completely fulfilling as that one, and for that I give infinite thanks.

The Eleventh Circle
The Lightness of Simplicity

The eleventh circle of wisdom is about the fresh possibilities and freedom to be discovered in simplicity; it is the wisdom of simplifying life in order to make it lighter, to free up time, space, and energy for exploring and delving further into the larger possibilities and meanings of life.

To live simply is to live with clear, uncomplicated purpose and vision. It is an ongoing process of uncovering and cutting through the extraneous, the unnecessary, and the frivolous in order to return to what is essential and of true import. It is finally being able to grow out of those aspects of life that can limit and contract our lives and to discover what truly matters.

Henry David Thoreau expresses this wisdom of living simply in the words "I wanted to live deep and suck out all the marrow of life." One of his greatest fears, he writes, was to find himself at the end of his days having not really lived at all, having lived a life mostly at the surface, with no real meaning or value in a larger sense. Along these same lines, Thoreau also said (the brief version): "The price of anything is the amount of life you have to pay for it."

To begin to simplify requires the motivation to continually bring awareness to bear on those areas of disharmony and suffering in life, to ask why, and to root out and transform those limitations. In this way simplicity is also about balance. It requires learning to prioritize and decide what matters most, to make the day-to-day choices that help to eliminate and subtract what is superfluous, and to bring into awareness the kernels of truth that remain. Living simply comes down to the wisest use of our limited time and life energy. It is deciding to search for and live in accord with a path that best harmonizes with our natural abilities, our visions and dreams—otherwise it becomes too easy to flounder and get lost in feelings of meaningless complication and to live without direction.

Simplicity, like the rest of the points on the circle of wisdom, is discovered, takes root, and grows in presence and in the light of all the other circles. To live simply is to learn to free oneself from the self-created and needless stress, worry, and fear that come with living outside of the Now and by being overly identified with a past and a future that exist only as thoughts, memories, and projections. We have the power of intelligent discernment. We can ask and decide if what we are doing at this moment is creating value for our individual lives, for others, and for life as a whole. If not, can we cut it out, change it, or simplify it in some way? This is an invaluable question, and it is one of the most important choices and actions we can make as human beings.

We know that people's notions vary about what living a simplified life means and how to create that life. Those beliefs depend on each individual's unique ability to handle varying levels of stress and complexity and what we believe is of genuine value and necessity. What is simple for one person will not necessarily be a simple way of living for another. Every person is different in this respect.

Moreover, some people may think adapting and living a simpler life looks good on paper but would be impossible in reality. There is a family to support, jobs to attend to, relationships, bills to pay, and endless other commitments that must come first, and that may make sense if there is still happiness and joy there. If not, then it may be time to start looking deeper, but each to their own and in their own time.

The best way I have found for beginning to create simplicity in life is to consistently ask specific questions that enable me to whittle away at the nonessential. Through this focused inquiry I can aspire to root out the trivial, the complicated, and the heavy, leaving only a simpler harmony and lightness of being and doing in its place. I call it the "trial of the true and essential." It involves simultaneously being the judge, the juror, and the plaintiff. Any form of the following questions can be helpful.

With the wisdom of Oneness and compassion in mind and heart, does this thing, these words, this act, this feeling or feelings add or contribute genuine value, beauty, health, and happiness to life in some way—mine and others? To the world as a whole?

Do my present thoughts, actions, and beliefs encourage a growth toward wholeness, add joy or meaning to the world? Do they complicate life or make it better? If not, how can I simplify or change whatever is being considered so that it lightens life, makes it more enjoyable and adds greater goodness to the world?

These are questions that at first glance may seem overly idealistic, but they can with patience and diligence be adapted to just about any facet of life that would benefit from simplification: all the clutter that crowds us, our homes and yards, our vehicles, finances, health, jobs, lifestyles, our use of technology, our relationships, living situations, our constantly thinking and planning minds, our visions and goals for life—and more.

Finally, it is important to remember that living a simple life is not about returning or regressing to some primitive or puritan state, bereft of the richness, improvements, and advantages of modern living. It doesn't mean to step back in time; instead, a life of intelligent simplicity is actually a higher, often more skillful and proficient way to live. It is a wisely informed efficiency that conserves and builds energy with less waste. With simplicity we discover the time and focus to change our lives and world for the better.

The Twelfth Circle
The Web and the Butterfly—Moving toward Planetary Oneness

The wisdom of the twelfth circle is the ever-growing realization that the differing degrees of Oneness felt and directly known during unity experiences are a mirror expression of the finite web of Oneness that is also the quintessential fabric of life on earth. Flow, wonder, high peak, and nondual states of consciousness all have the potential of opening the human totality, not only to Life as One and the source of existence, but also to the Oneness of life at a planetary level. They are ultimately one and the same.

Science demonstrates time and again that human beings are in ways seen and unseen, inseparable and one with the life-generative and -sustaining ecological and elemental matrix from which all life arises—the earth. A growing body of scientific research and data shows with increasing clarity and indisputability the true interconnectedness and wholeness of life. This big blue planet with its precious biosphere and all its many interdependent, interrelating, synergistic systems, living and nonliving, are what make life possible. We are already aware of this wisdom at some level, deep in our hearts and bones, because all life is a manifestation of that creative dynamic. Science simply verifies that common intuition in clear and definable ways.

The famous quote from Chief Seattle speaks this truth simply but eloquently: "Man did not weave the web of life; he is merely a strand in it. Whatever he does to the web, he does to himself."

I use the words "the web and the butterfly" as a heading because together they are fitting analogies for interconnectivity and Oneness. Most everyone has seen and knows what happens to a spider's web as it is being touched at one point—the whole web moves in response. There is a movement of energy as vibration from one point to all points, and it affects the whole in ways both obvious and imperceptible.

Likewise, the term "butterfly effect," used initially to express the unpredictability of weather patterns, is now a generalized metaphor for describing how small changes (and choices) will often transform into major, sometimes monumental changes over time and space. The energy of a butterfly's wing beat will ripple, spread, and slowly build its unseen effects—ultimately playing a part in a hurricane on the other side of the planet. These are both perfect images for the earth-scale ecological imbalance that is upon us now.

The path that we continue to follow as a species is steadily and with increasing impact contributing to the impoverishment, depletion, and homogenization of our planet's biological and ecological treasures. The health of life on earth is utterly dependent on the richness of the connections and the number of possibilities that are available to it, but our shortsighted choices are slowly but surely diminishing our planet's incredible diversity and the stabilizing cohesiveness that diversity provides. Unfortunately, these negative, large-scale environmental changes can be easily overlooked or ignored in a human's relatively short life span—to a point that is.

Human exploitation and development with only short-term immediate gain in mind is leading to enormous long-term, nonreversible losses and destruction. It makes absolutely no sense that we are continuing to make these choices as a species, yet we are all part of it in some way. It seems to be old news for many these days and relegated to the shadows. The present political situation in the United States is an excellent example of that direction in thought and concern. We continue to defecate in our one and only home. The poisons are building—in our bodies, where we live and work, and everywhere we go. No one can hide; no one is exempt.

It's as if humanity as a whole is stuck in a pathological, male-dominated adolescent level of arrested development: resistant to change, impulsive, isolated, disconnected, and violent—unable to truly grasp the bigger picture, to understand and act out of true compassion and unitive wisdom. Of course, there are many amazing exceptions out there, people and groups that care deeply and work every day to change things for the better. But despite those human powers in our favor, one thing is undeniably clear and certain: It will take a major shift in consciousness to really change to the degree that is called for now. The "paradigm shift" that we need more than ever continues to elude us. As Einstein said so wisely, "No problem can be solved from the same level of consciousness that created it."

The consciousness that must be changed is the continued lack of foresight and compassion for both present and future generations, the same obsessed self-interest that arises out of an ego-centered, divisive consciousness. Consciousness at that level continues to propagate and reinforce a belief in a need for more—more wealth, power, accumulation, and control, along with an unrestrained and unbalanced development at any cost. This, of course, is nothing new, and that's the problem and the challenge. If we don't grow beyond this destructive mindset, if we don't learn to grow into a more integrative and caring state of consciousness, nothing will change sufficiently for genuine transformation to occur.

For me that change means learning to understand the parts—how they relate, connect, and affect one another—but all the while attempting to stay rooted in the wisdom of Oneness and the bigger picture. So much of this book is about the "bigger picture." It is learning to make wisely informed decisions every day, in line with our shared unitive wisdom. It requires a shift from exclusively thinking and acting in parts to living from a base and center of wholeness.

Education, as I think most will agree, is usually one of the most important first steps to any endeavor of this nature. It is an education and change of consciousness that involves not only learning the particulars—the how, what, when, where, and why of making smart and meaningful ecological choices—but also the larger vision of moving toward a more unitive form of consciousness by learning how to wake up and grow up in our own unique ways.

One of the most effective and impactful ways we can act is through the tremendous influence we have in how and where we spend our money. Corporations change quickly if they know the market demands it. It sounds simple, but it is a powerfully effective and influential choice if enacted. It takes a sustained and consistent effort to learn about and make wisely informed, ecologically minded choices consistently, and sometimes there just are no good options available. Or the ones that are out there are not economically feasible. Then it becomes a matter of becoming creative.

I am definitely not speaking from a pedestal here. It has been and continues to be a constant challenge for me to keep informed, make the right decisions, and not get lazy. There are good days and bad days, but the broader vision and aspiration are there. The wise counsel held in the *thirteen circles of timeless wisdom,* along with the unifying power of experiences of Oneness are that source of inspiration and motivation for me now.

Ironically, choosing an attitude of doom and gloom is simply another form of an ego-based reaction; it is buying into and identifying with another collective drama. The other choice is to learn to see and act from a "self-expanded," integrative intelligence that moves realistically, creatively, and imaginatively toward a wiser future for all life and for the whole planet. The web is becoming increasingly unstable and the butterfly's effect is becoming stronger. We need the wisdom of Oneness like never before.

The Thirteenth Circle
The Wisdom of Our Mortality
and the Cosmic Kaleidoscope

One of life's greatest mysteries is its inevitable end. We grow, we age, and we die; we know in our depths that sooner or later that ending will arrive, even if outwardly we ignore it, resist it, or attempt to defy it. Death and change, particularly in a biological sense, are life's two certainties—irrefutable and absolute.

But as humans we have the amazing faculty to be aware of this circular dance of life and death in a reflective and intelligent way. Yet this self-aware intelligence can also be a double-edged sword: The awareness of our looming mortality can potentially be the source of a continual, low-level, often subterranean fear and angst, especially if it is never examined and brought to the light of consciousness. The wisdom of the thirteenth circle is learning to become increasingly conscious of that mortality, not as a source of anxiety or morbid resignation, but as a means of truly empowering our lives and choices. Life is precious, and it is the fact of life's certain end that makes it so much more so.

The first time I was exposed to the idea of death as a positive and complementary side of life was while reading the Carlos Castaneda book *Journey to Ixtlan*. I had never encountered anything like it, and it has stuck with me ever since. The shaman Don Juan says to his apprentice Carlos:

"Focus your attention on the link between you and your death, without remorse or sadness or worrying. Focus your attention on the fact that you don't have time and let your acts flow accordingly. Let each of your acts be your last battle on earth. Only under those conditions will your acts have their rightful power. Otherwise they will be, for as long as you live, the acts of a timid man."

Don Juan continues on,

"But if you are going to die there is no time for timidity, simply because timidity makes you cling to something that exists only in your thoughts. It soothes you while everything is at a lull, but then the awesome, mysterious world will open its mouth for you, as it will for every one of us, and then you will realize that your sure ways were not that sure at all. Being timid prevents us from [exploring and realizing the greater possibilities of our lives.]"

These words epitomize the wisdom of the thirteenth circle in such a vivid and emotionally stirring way. I was sixteen when I first read them and I was blown away. It was the perfect time for me to have read them. The images and feelings conjured and brought to life by those passages had an immediate and lasting effect on me. It was actually liberating in some unexpected way. It changed me.

Each expression of life is a wondrously unique and creative unfurling of possibility never seen before, never to be seen again. So what we do, what we create with our lives matters in the most profound way. We never know when the final seconds of this inimitable life will be upon us. It is that uncertainty, that unknown that is the mystery of mysteries, and it is our power. A balanced and wise awareness of our mortality and of the limits of life given to us by death can become an ever-present and available balancer and equalizer for life—a reference point. It is a way to clear away and see through and beyond the extraneous; it is a means and a reminder to get at the heart of what matters most in life.

An intentional consciousness of death becomes a tool for cutting out the petty, for simplifying, for learning to let go of burdensome attachments and a way to become humble, big-minded, and loving—knowing that our ends are assured and unforeseeable. In this light, the common expression "to live each day as if it were your last" becomes much clearer and empowering, not a reason for fear but as a source of inspiration and motivation.

A big-picture awareness of death is the perfect way to create a larger, more accepting, and inclusive perspective. It is a way to remember that a life caught in the shallows and of ego-generated drama and self-importance ends up wasting an exorbitant amount of time, energy, and potential. We truly cannot take any of the possessions, ideas, dreams, and achievements, the accumulated wealth, or any of the other roles and coverings of life with us in the end. Our mortality cuts those surface layers off like a guillotine.

Yet from a larger perspective, it would make sense that some part of us, as mirrors of the greater whole, moves on and continues to transform and evolve in ways unknown. Some of us feel this to be true in a profoundly intuitive way. And what I am referring to here is not the idea of some kind of disembodied soul or spirit that carries on our self-identity. It is my feeling that this mind-generated identity dies with the body. But I do sense, given the cyclical and evolving patterns of nature, that there is a continuation somehow of the nonphysical energy that vitalizes our beings during life—in the same way that our physical energies carry on in the material world we leave behind.

This intuited continuity is articulated in an eloquent and moving way in this poem, "Do Not Stand at My Grave and Weep," written in 1932 by Mary Elizabeth Frye.

> Do not stand at my grave and weep
> I am not there. I do not sleep.
> I am a thousand winds that blow.
> I am the diamond glints on snow.
> I am the sunlight on ripened grain.
> I am the gentle autumn rain.
> When you awaken in the morning's hush
> I am the swift uplifting rush
> Of quiet birds in circled flight.
> I am the soft stars that shine at night.
> Do not stand at my grave and cry;
> I am not there. I did not die.

Death is truly the great and final transformer; it is the ultimate unity experience. The human wave of our metaphor breaks open and falls back into the infinity of the Ocean of Oneness, in the same way that our human "beingness" returns to the ground of infinite Being, finite life returns to Infinite Life.

Different cultures, religions, and spiritual traditions may have strong beliefs about what happens to an individual's consciousness after the death of the physical body. Scientists, Buddhists, Muslims, Hindus, Christians, atheists, agnostics, people who have had near-death experiences, and most everyone else have some opinion or feeling about the matter as well, even if it is simply the belief in total and complete oblivion, nothingness, or perhaps no belief at all. In the final hour though, death is the greatest of mysteries and nobody knows for sure what it holds.

My intuition is that in some way there is an element of truth to all of these different beliefs about life and death in terms of how these hugely important parts and interpretations of reality are eventually realized. As in waking life, the deeply held beliefs and feelings we hold about how our lives and the universe work ultimately affect to a large degree how our lives and deaths actually unfold. The transformation that occurs in death may somehow happen in much the same way—as a reflection of what we "believe" about death in life. Our universe seems to be a true mystery and cosmic house of mirrors at times.

The Cosmic Kaleidoscope—The Big, Big Picture

Part of the final circle of the thirteen circles of unitive wisdom is a return to the center and Source. It is the wisdom of opening and staying open to the universal human intelligence of our deepest being—what Carl Jung referred to as the collective unconscious. In our most profound depths we all share an ancient and instinctive knowledge that continually informs our lives in ways seen and unseen, known and unknown. It is the unifying and integrative wisdom expressed in the universal symbols of Life as both infinite and finite—the stories, dreams, archetypes, and myths that offer light in the darkness, a path through the darkest of forests—like the mythical hero's journey of self-discovery.

The enacted wisdom of this last circle is learning to intentionally stay aware of and in touch with this rich subterranean wellspring of insight and meaning. It is remembering to tune in to this potential source of guiding wisdom through increasing presence and awareness, through attention to dreams, through stories and imagination, by listening with our whole being and by shining the light of consciousness on those aspects of our lives that often lie in the shadows, below and beyond our everyday awareness.

Looked at from within the metaphor of the Ocean of Oneness and its waves, the mysterious and bottomless vastness below the Ocean's surface is symbolic of this great unknown. By envisioning those ineffable depths we might imagine the enormity that lies outside of consciousness. I metaphorically call these depths the Cosmic Kaleidoscope. It is another way of making graspable the incomprehensible dynamic at the heart of our human reality and universe to which those myths, stories, and dreams mentioned above help connect us.

Remember the childhood delight of peering into a kaleidoscope's beautiful world of glimmering, luminescent, swirling forms of color and light. Through this revolving telescope of metal and glass a vision of vital, flowing color and shape is seen being created and recreated anew each moment and with every turn. Energy and color continually transform into a circular stream of ever-novel, interconnected patterns.

In a similar way, life, earth, and the universe can also be imagined; they are all an interconnected web of energy, of interrelating and unifying patterns of matter, space, energy, light, awareness, and form manifesting and interacting throughout all levels of existence. Our universe is an immensity of kaleidoscopic mirrors, patterns within patterns, reflected on and on at a multitude of scales, from the subatomic to the cosmic, informing and unforming all reality. It is the holographic and fractal nature of our universe: The One that is reflected in each and all, and each and all a reflection of the greater whole.

The universe as we've come to know and understand it is rooted in and arises out of these kaleidoscopic depths that perpetually inform and transform reality. It is similar to the Eastern concept of karma but vastly expanded. It is way beyond cause and effect; it is the ripple effect *ad infinitum*, affecting and influencing not only human reality, but the entire universe.

When we die, the wave of our individual life unfurls, releases, and returns home to its source: the greater Ocean of Being. The energy that coursed through and vitalized the life and awareness of that particular wave returns like a drop of water to the Ocean, rippling throughout and changing in ways small and large all of existence, like the butterfly's fluttering wings of the previous circle but on a universal scale and beyond. This grander vision and understanding has the potential to change everything in terms of how we as human beings relate to each other and to the world as a whole. Our lives now become infused with true meaning and a deeper purpose.

Everything, every single detail of our lives makes a difference, not in the limited and relative sense of being judged as good or bad, but in relation to playing an invaluable and unrepeatable part in the bigger cosmic picture of Oneness and evolution. Once more it can be likened to the innumerable notes of an unfathomably immense symphony. Each note, although only a tiny part of the whole, matters and adds something indispensable. The potential of creating increasing degrees of harmony through Oneness and love is our greatest possibility as conscious beings. We have a choice. All that we are, all that we have done or will do, all that we have experienced becomes an infinitesimal but absolutely essential turning and rippling of that Cosmic Kaleidoscope. Nothing is lost.

Living the Wisdom

An obvious and relevant question that comes to mind with respect to the thirteen circles of wisdom is how to make that wisdom not only an intellectual aspect of our lives, but more important, how to make it a lived and experiential reality. All of the unitive wisdom held within the circle is a profound and cohesive expression of the wisdom arising out of the hearts, souls, intellects, and intuitions of countless humans, remembered and forgotten, over thousands of years of human life. Each point is intimately interconnected to and interwoven with all others; each arises inseparable from and interdependent on the other.

In other words, growing in one point of wisdom will invariably help one to grow in all other points. The thirteen circles of wisdom is a tapestry of interrelationships that continually influence one another. It is circular synergy, a circle of mirrored points of wisdom and knowledge reflecting one another as a whole. And all circles emerge from the center point—Life's unlimited possibilities.

With that in mind, my own approach to making this wisdom a lived and waking reality is to charge each point with clear and vital energy, will, attention, and intention every single day, in as many ways as possible. The overall vision is to make each and all of them a "living truth," a powerfully lived presence and a walked talk. If I'm going to have thoughts going through my head anyway, it makes sense to take a deliberate and intelligent part in choosing and enacting those thoughts.

What that has meant for me in terms of a practical path is to absorb the wisdom of the circles so deeply, so thoroughly that I ooze, sweat, and emanate that wisdom. To do that I write about them, read about them, imagine, visualize, talk about, and memorize each point so that I no longer have to think about what each point of wisdom means. I know them "by heart," mind, body, and spirit. This is an ongoing and building progression; there is always more to learn, to include, and to integrate.

Often I imagine and visualize each point of wisdom in the most vivid and strongly felt ways possible—sensing it, feeling it, knowing it to be an actual and present reality. One practice that has helped a great deal is to run through each circle from start to finish like a story that I am telling myself that is already true and genuinely felt. Each time I tell this story in the images of mind and heart it is slightly different and affects me in a different way. It is a powerful tool.

The nature of mind is thought. How we direct and focus that thought is our decision. We can choose to embody and act from a center of presence, with the wisdom of Oneness, letting our thoughts, feelings, and actions be guided by those innate possibilities. We can continue growing up and waking up to more unifying and compassionate spheres of awareness, or we can remain stuck in a consciousness that is trapped and stunted by the gravitational pull of an unexamined, separative, conditioning that we too often allow to limit our lives. Once more—our power is our choice, our choice is our power.

Chapter 7
The End
That Is a Beginning

As you hopefully see now, experiences of Oneness can be true life changers; they are states that come and go, but they have the potential to transform our lives in an unforgettable and lasting way if given attention, welcomed, and understood. Unity experiences, from the smallest taste to the most expansive, are glimpses of an infinite puzzle, and life is about discovering and learning how to put all those seemingly separate pieces together, the many parts that make us unique, but also that make us one.

At some level and at some point, we will be called to answer to that strong or subtle urge to seek outwardly for the truth that in reality lies within. And even though we may read and be told that the truth revealed in "knowing oneself" is an inner journey, life must still be lived and experienced firsthand, outwardly and in the world—until we finally see that the inside and the outside are one, that the starting and ending point are the same. As expressed many times and in many ways: the spirit of life, of the universe itself, is an orchestrated, spiraling dance of discovery, growth, and the exploration of endless possibilities. It is an experience of losing oneself and hopefully finding one's way to a greater and wiser understanding of Oneness and love.

Despite the powerful forces in today's world that often discourage the growth of human possibility toward a more unifying and holistic consciousness, I believe that it is still an inherent tendency and heartfelt aspiration for humans to relate to one other and the world in a more unified way. At some level, we all have a deep desire to grow, to make life better for ourselves and for others, to find wholeness and connectedness. The weak link in this growth process is allowing ourselves to become so mired in our own self-centeredness and selfishness that we eventually become too conditioned and lost, too heavy and apathetic to think we can change—or worse, not to care anymore.

Experiences of Oneness are one of the keys for unlocking our higher potential and for rising above a dispirited path of disconnect and apathy. I know without a doubt that unity experiences are some of the most important possibilities in our lives. Again, they are clues that have the capacity to empower our lives with meaning, beauty, wonder, and joy like nothing else, but they must be integrated into the totality of life—body, mind, heart, and spirit.

To reiterate, this knowledge, these ideas are not mine or any one particular person's. It is a collective, accumulated wisdom built up by millions of individuals over time, like the solitary yet unified polyps of a coral reef building gigantic reef structures over millions of years. This priceless unitive wisdom belongs to all of us, and *The Possibilities of Oneness* is simply my interpretation and understanding of that unifying wisdom.

The beauty is that no one has to take my or anyone else's word for it. This is a pathway of discovery and integration that can be tested, experimented with, examined, and validated by anyone and everyone, independently, with others, and together. We can see if this wisdom holds value, truth, and meaning for us and then make a choice based on that exploration. We have the power to decide whether or not to continue along the road of those possibilities. Moreover, it makes no difference what culture, religion, spiritual tradition, or belief system a person may belong or adhere to—some aspect of this human wisdom will offer the potential for transformation and higher human understanding regardless of those beliefs or culture.

As I said, sadly this kind of growth is not necessarily supported or consistently encouraged in our times. It goes against the grain of that imbalanced, mostly male-dominated, egocentric, greed-and power-driven view of life that has somehow become so prevalent in today's world. It is a worldview that both emerges from and perpetuates a hardline scientific materialism, consumerism, political polarity, social and economic injustices, and a sometimes closed-minded and biased media pushing fear like a shot of adrenaline, oblivious to the long-term consequences.

After all, it is much easier to manipulate and control people caught up in the hypnotic effects and herd mentality of a consciousness limited and clouded by insecurity and the belief in an isolated self with endless needs and desires. It is the perennially dangling promise of the "good life" that continually lures us and is used to shape, direct, and influence society and keep the world's economic machine running. In the end, we must ask ourselves what living the good life really means.

And by no means has it slipped my mind that a major portion of the human population still lacks access to even the most basic needs, let alone the time, energy, and resources to pursue growth. This too is one of the underlying motivations for writing *The Possibilities of Oneness*: to add another voice to our dire need for real and lasting change, for a transformation toward a more unifying, compassionate, and wiser foundation of consciousness. We must join together, become a collective force, a single unstoppable wave of change, and direct our attention and energies toward the creation of this new reality. If we don't find a way to do this soon, our same old road will become progressively more uncertain and unstable. Sure, technology can and will help, but not if our biosphere has been pushed beyond certain limits. Consciousness is the key, not scientific and materialistic advancement. A growing and robust economy is only important if, and only if, there is a healthy and whole human awareness, planet, and biosphere to support it.

It's unbelievable at times to think of the progress we have made as a species, in so many different areas of life: increasing rights, justice, equality, liberties, technology, science, ecological and environmental awareness, and legislation, every area of human knowledge and much more. But along with those achievements there has also been a largely ego-driven shadow side: war, holocaust, and genocide, millions of senseless deaths, violence, destruction, and environmental degradation on a planetary level. The challenges that remain are enormous, but our potential to answer those challenges is more powerful still.

We all on occasion, even if rarely, have the sense that something is missing in our lives. We try in many different ways to fill the space, but we are seldom able to fully satiate the restlessness, the edginess, the subtle or heavy sadness, the feeling that something more seems to always be just around the corner. Those are the whispers urging us to explore the more meaningful depths of life. Unity experiences are doorways into those deep waters, into the vastness of the human heart, spirit, and into the Infinity that is the very source of the universe itself. The mystery of existence is barely touched by thought; the possibilities are extraordinary.

In the light and in the darkness, the meaningful questions of Life both big and small are already deep within us, born with us, hidden and unformed—waiting. The right questions will reveal themselves if we choose to listen in silence and with our whole being. In that stilled and emptied presence, answers will also emerge and gradually become clearer. It is within our power to grow out of the separative and fragmenting consciousness that is decimating and impoverishing the health and life of our planet and into a unifying and integrative one. With the possibilities and wisdom of Oneness, we have the potential to truly take humanity to the next higher, wiser, inspired, and compassionate circle on the spiral of human and cosmic evolution. That is my deepest desire, vision, and hope—the beginning.

Notes

Chapter 1–What Is Oneness?

1. Albert Einstein, "Letter of 1950," as quoted by *New York Times* (March 29, 1972).

Chapter 4–Experiences of Oneness from My Life

1. Duane Elgin, *The Living Universe* (San Francisco, CA: Berrett-Koehler Publisher, Inc., 2009), 102-103.
2. Thomas Merton, *No Man Is an Island* (New York, NY: Mariner Books, 2002).

Chapter 5–Oneness as Understood and Experienced by Others

1. Tom Robbins, *Tibetan Peach Pie* (New York, NY: HarperCollins Publishers, 2014), 89.
2. Duane Elgin, *The Living Universe* (San Francisco, CA: Berrett-Koehler Publisher, Inc., 2009), 81.
3. Elgin, *The Living Universe*, 167.
4. Alan Watts, *The Wisdom of Insecurity* (New York, NY: Random House, 1951), 53.
5. Watts, *The Wisdom of Insecurity*, 112.
6. Alan Watts, *The Book* (New York, NY: Random House, 1966), 13.
7. Diane K. Osbon, *A Joseph Campbell Companion* (New York, NY: HarperCollins Publishers, 1991), 164.

8. Charlotte Joko Beck, *Everyday Zen* (New York, NY: HarperCollins Publishers, 1989), 126.
9. Lucy Oliver, *The Meditator's Guidebook* (Rochester, Vermont: Destiny Books, 1991), 16.
10. Thomas Cleary, trans., *Zen Essence—The Science of Freedom* (Boston, Massachusetts: Shambhala Publications, 1989), 60.
11. Ken Keys Jr., *Handbook to Higher Consciousness* (Coos Bay, Oregon: The Living Loving Center, 1975), 80.
12. Ken Wilber, *The Eye of Spirit* (Boston, Massachusetts: Shambhala Publications, 1997), 283.
13. Walter Truett Anderson, *The Next Enlightenment* (New York, NY: St. Martin's Press, 2003), 205.
14. Sam Harris, *Waking Up* (New York, NY: Simon & Schuster Paperbacks, 2014), 81.
15. Eckhart Tolle, *A New Earth* (New York, NY: Penguin Group/Dutton, 2005), 115.
16. Shunryu Suzuki, *Zen Mind, Beginner's Mind* (New York, NY: John Weatherhill, Inc.), 94.
17. Marsha Sinetar, *Ordinary People as Monks and Mystics* (Mahwah, New Jersey: Paulist Press, 1986), 93.
18. Sinetar, *Ordinary People*, 95.
19. Marilyn Schlitz, Cassandra Vieten, and Tina Amorok, *Living Deeply* (Oakland, CA: New Harbinger Publications, 2007), 45.
20. Schlitz et al., *Living Deeply*, 58.
21. Martin Luther King Jr., "Letter from Birmingham Jail," in *Why We Can't Wait* (Boston, Massachusetts: Beacon Press, 1963) 77-100.
22. Vivekananda, *Living at the Source, Yoga Teachings of Vivekananda* (Boston, Massachusetts: Shambhala Publications, 1993), 38.
23. John Greer, *Seeing, Knowing, Being* (Memphis, Tennessee: True Compass Press, 2012), 4.
24. Martha Orton, *Oneness* (Bloomington, IN: iUniverse, 2013), 3.

25. Eckhart Tolle, *The Power of Now* (Novato, CA: New World Library, 1999), 10.

26. Leo Tolstoy, *War and Peace*, Constance Garnett, trans. (New York, NY: Random House, 1979), 141.

27. Pierre Teilhard de Chardin, *The Phenomenon of Man* (New York, NY: Harper & Row, 1959).

28. Brian Swimme and Thomas Berry, *The Universe Story* (New York, NY: HarperCollins Publishers, 1992), 21.

29. J. Krishnamurti, *The Flame of Attention* (New York, NY: HarperCollins Publishers, 1984), 50.

Chapter 6–Thirteen Circles of Timeless Wisdom

1. Henry David Thoreau, 1817-1862. Excerpt taken from *Walden*; originally published in 1854.

2. Carlos Castaneda, *Journey to Ixtlan* (New York, NY: Simon & Schuster, 1972), 84-85.

3. Mary Elizabeth Frye, "Do Not Stand at My Grave and Weep," (1932). Found on https://www.poemhunter.com/poem/do-not-stand-at-my-grave-and-weep/. Original version.

Acknowledgments

In light of the expansive vision I've attempted to explore in this book, another entire volume could have been written to acknowledge all the innumerable influences that ripple throughout this personal and collective story of Oneness. I'm profoundly grateful for all of it, to everyone, known and unknown, seen and unseen.

In particular and to some of those present in each page of this book: I thank the wise experience and suggestions of my editors, Betsy Robinson and Kendra Langeteig and to my proofreader, Joni Wilson.

Warm thanks as well to Deborah Perdue from Illumination Graphics for her years of design experience and skill—and for her monumental patience.

To friends and family for their encouragement and for asking how it was going along the way, I thank you.

And finally, a heartfelt thank you to Vicki for her caring support, her gentle kindness, and the beautiful shine she adds to my life every day.

About the Author

Will Irons has been an avid explorer of the World's Wisdom Traditions for more than three decades. He has degrees in philosophy and nursing and has worked as a science teacher and a naturalist. Irons has also been a dedicated practitioner of presence-centered meditation for many years—mostly discovered and cultivated in the wild places of Colorado these days. He served for two years in Panama, Central America, as a volunteer in the Peace Corps, where he taught environmental education and wrote a marine environmental education teaching guide in collaboration with the Smithsonian Tropical Research Institute. Irons presently lives and writes in Fort Collins, Colorado.

www.ingramcontent.com/pod-product-compliance
Lightning Source LLC
Chambersburg PA
CBHW021124300426
44113CB00006B/276